About This Book

Why is this topic important?

A well-trained workforce is essential for success in a competitive global economy. Yet even though training requires a wide range of knowledge and skills, people with little or no training experience are often called upon to develop and conduct training programs. People who are new to training and those with limited experience need easily accessible information that helps them understand what training is all about, along with practical tools they can use immediately to design, develop, and conduct successful training programs.

What can you achieve with this book?

In the 21st Century organization, people who are new to training do not have the luxury of time in which to learn about the various instructional design methods, adult learning theories, and approaches to teaching. This book is an easy-to-use resource that provides practical information, best practices, proven strategies, tips, and tools for meeting the challenges of today's fast-paced, rapidly changing learning environment.

How is this book organized?

The first two chapters provide an overview of what training is, what trainers do, and how adults learn. Chapters 3 through 6 cover the basics of instructional design, the ways in which training is delivered, and the process of developing, delivering, and evaluating training, while Chapter 7 provides a look at the terminology commonly used in the field. The last chapter discusses what's involved in becoming a training professional. Each chapter includes questions and application activities to enhance learning. At the back of the book is a list of resources.

About Pfeiffer

Pfeiffer serves the professional development and hands-on resource needs of training and human resource practitioners and gives them products to do their jobs better. We deliver proven ideas and solutions from experts in HR development and HR management, and we offer effective and customizable tools to improve workplace performance. From novice to seasoned professional, Pfeiffer is the source you can trust to make yourself and your organization more successful.

Essential Knowledge   Pfeiffer produces insightful, practical, and comprehensive materials on topics that matter the most to training and HR professionals. Our Essential Knowledge resources translate the expertise of seasoned professionals into practical, how-to guidance on critical workplace issues and problems. These resources are supported by case studies, worksheets, and job aids and are frequently supplemented with CD-ROMs, websites, and other means of making the content easier to read, understand, and use.

Essential Tools   Pfeiffer's Essential Tools resources save time and expense by offering proven, ready-to-use materials—including exercises, activities, games, instruments, and assessments—for use during a training or team-learning event. These resources are frequently offered in looseleaf or CD-ROM format to facilitate copying and customization of the material.

Pfeiffer also recognizes the remarkable power of new technologies in expanding the reach and effectiveness of training. While e-hype has often created whizbang solutions in search of a problem, we are dedicated to bringing convenience and enhancements to proven training solutions. All our e-tools comply with rigorous functionality standards. The most appropriate technology wrapped around essential content yields the perfect solution for today's on-the-go trainers and human resource professionals.

Essential resources for training and HR professionals

www.pfeiffer.com

Training Fundamentals

Pfeiffer Essential Guides to Training Basics

Janis Fisher Chan

A Wiley Imprint
www.pfeiffer.com

Library of Congress Cataloging-in-Publication Data

Chan, Janis Fisher.
    Training fundamentals/Janis Fisher Chan.
       p.   cm. — (Pfeiffer essential guides to training basics)
    Includes bibliographical references and index.
    ISBN 978-0-470-40468-3 (pbk.)
       1. Employees —Training of.   2. Employee training personnel.   3. Training.   I. Title.
HF5549.5.T7C534 2010
658.3'124—dc22
                                                                                        2009031947

Acquiring Editor: Matthew Davis   Editorial Assistant: Lindsay Morton
Director of Development: Kathleen Dolan Davies   Manufacturing Supervisor: Becky Morgan
Production Editor: Dawn Kilgore
Editor: Rebecca Taff

Printed in the United States of America

Printing   10 9 8 7 6 5 4 3 2 1

Contents

Introduction

An acting teacher I know once asked his class of professional actors, "Why do you do this work? It's hard, it's frustrating, and it demands all your attention. What keeps you going?" After a moment of silence, one student said, "Because it's more fun than anything I've ever done."

That's how I sometimes feel about training. It's hard work. It's frustrating. It demands a lot of attention. But it's more challenging and exciting than any other work I've done. It forces me to draw on all my knowledge, and all my skills. It has transformed me into a lifelong learner. It continually surprises me.

Like so many others in the field, I never set out to become a training professional. When I began, I hardly knew what training was or what a trainer did. I learned on the job (a time-honored form of training), designing and conducting training programs before I knew any of the theories about how adults learn, discovering what worked through trial and error (another way in which people learn). It wasn't until I'd been in the field for quite a while that I learned how much valuable information was available from professional organizations, books, and experienced trainers.

In this book and the other two books in the *Training Basics* series, I've tried to share with you some of what I and other training professionals have learned about how to provide training that achieves results for individuals and their organizations. These books do not attempt to cover everything you need or want to know—there's far too much information, far too many theories, too many ideas and strategies for that. But they do provide an introduction to the training world that will help you get started. When you're ready to learn more, you'll find a wealth of resources out there to help you grow and develop in your career.

About the Pfeiffer Essential Guides to Training Basics

The three books in this series, *Training Fundamentals, Designing and Developing Training Programs*, and *Delivering Training Workshops*, provide practical ideas, information, tips, and techniques for people who are new to training as

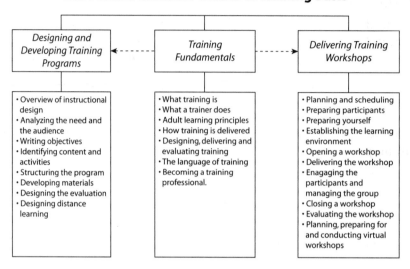

The Pfeiffer Essential Guides to Training Basis

Designing and Developing Training Programs	Training Fundamentals	Delivering Training Workshops
• Overview of instructional design • Analyzing the need and the audience • Writing objectives • Identifying content and activities • Structuring the program • Developing materials • Designing the evaluation • Designing distance learning	• What training is • What a trainer does • Adult learning principles • How training is delivered • Designing, delivering and evaluating training • The language of training • Becoming a training professional.	• Planning and scheduling • Preparing participants • Preparing yourself • Establishing the learning environment • Opening a workshop • Delivering the workshop • Enagaging the participants and managing the group • Closing a workshop • Evaluating the workshop • Planning, preparing for and conducting virtual workshops

well as trainers who have been in the field for a while and would like to learn more.

Training Fundamentals

This book is a no-nonsense, practical overview of training. Here's what you'll learn:

- What training is and the role it plays in helping organizations achieve their goals
- What a trainer does and the characteristics and skills a trainer needs to be successful
- The ways in which training is delivered
- The adult learning principles that guide successful training programs
- What's involved in designing training to meet specific needs, delivering training workshops, and evaluating training success
- The terminology and acronyms commonly used in the training field
- How you can develop yourself as a training professional

Designing and Developing Training

Building on the basics provided in *Training Fundamentals*, this book guides you through the instructional design process, providing practical ideas, information, tools, and strategies you can use immediately. You'll learn how to:

- Make sure that training is needed, relevant, and cost-effective
- Analyze the needs and characteristics of the audience
- Write the behavioral learning objectives that form the foundation of a training program
- Decide what content to include
- Select activities that engage people and help them learn
- Organize content and activities into a workable structure
- Develop trainer guides, participant workbooks, slide presentations, and other learning materials
- Design a program evaluation
- Design virtual and remote training programs

Delivering Training Workshops

Also building on the basics of delivery presented in *Training Fundamentals*, this book provides strategies, best practices, tips, and guidelines you can use immediately to prepare for, deliver, and follow up a workshop. You'll learn how to:

- Plan and schedule a workshop
- Prepare participants so they know what to expect and arrive ready to learn
- Increase your confidence by preparing yourself to conduct training
- Establish an environment that is conducive to learning
- Get started in a way that immediately engages participants
- Present information clearly, keep people involved, and respond to questions
- Manage the group and keep the workshop on track
- Close a workshop in a way that helps participants use what they learn
- Evaluate the success of a workshop
- Plan, prepare for, and conduct virtual workshops

How to Use This Book

This book is designed as a learning tool. You'll find questions and suggested activities that will help you think about what you are learning, make connections between new learning and what you already know, and apply what you learn. The answers to the questions are either apparent in the text or appear at the end of the chapter. I encourage you to answer the questions and do the activities, but feel free to skip any that don't seem relevant. In other words, this is your book; use it the way that works best for you.

Check What You Know
When you see this icon, you'll find questions that help you see what you already know about the topic or subtopic.

THINK ABOUT IT

When you see this icon, you'll find questions that help you think about something that you have learned.

Quick Quiz
From time to time, you'll find a quiz that will help you check your understanding of the material.

Apply What You Learn

When you see this icon, you'll find questions or an activity to help you apply the learning to a real situation.

Before You Begin

One theme that you'll find throughout the *Training Basics* series is the importance of helping people apply what they learn in training to real-world situations. That's the purpose of the activities that most of the chapters—to help you apply the learning to a training project of your own.

Choose a project that you can think about as you read this book and describe it below. The project should be a training program that you need to develop and/or one that you need to deliver. If you have no real, current project to work on, think of a training program that you could provide for people at your company or for people at another organization, such as a nonprofit or community group.

Briefly describe your training program:

_____

_____

Who is the audience for this program?

_____

_____

Why is this program needed? What is it intended to accomplish?

_____

_____

_____

_____

Your Objectives

Another important theme that you will find in each book of the series is that it's easier to get somewhere when you know where you are going. Think about what you would like to accomplish by reading this book and briefly describe your objectives below:

_____

_____

_____

_____

_____

_____

_____

_____

_____

_____

_____

_____

_____

_____

_____

_____

1

An Introduction to Training

Check What You Know

"I'm thinking about changing jobs," Justin told his colleague Rachael as they left their building to attend a meeting.

"I thought you liked your work," Rachael said.

"I do. But there's a trainer position opening up in the Learning and Human Performance Department, and my manager said that she'd support me if I wanted to apply for it. She knows that I'm looking for something more challenging, and that I'd like more opportunities to work with people."

"So you'd be teaching?"

"That's part of it. But according to the job description, it involves lots of other things, too."

They reached the door of the meeting room. "When do you have to decide?" Rachael asked.

"The application deadline is next Thursday. But I need to find out a lot more about training before I can figure out whether I've got what it takes and whether it would be the right move for me. At this point, all I've got is an idea and a list of questions."

(Continued)

What could you tell Justin about training? Some of his questions are below. How would you answer them?

1. What is training? Is it the same thing as education? What are the key differences?

   _____

   _____

   _____

   _____

2. What's the primary purpose of a training program?

   _____

   _____

   _____

3. What does a trainer do? What are a trainer's roles and responsibilities?

   _____

   _____

   _____

   _____

4. What skills and characteristics does a trainer need?

   _____

   _____

   _____

   _____

By the time we enter the workforce, we've spent years in the classroom. We know how to do research, study, take tests, and write papers. We have learned a little about a lot of subjects, and a lot about a few subjects. We have learned how to do many things, a few of them very well. All that education has provided us with a good foundation for living our lives and launching our careers. But learning doesn't stop when we leave school. In fact, few of us could do our jobs on the basis of our education alone. For us to become proficient at our work and productive members of our organizations, and to continue developing our careers, there is a great deal more that we need to learn. That's where training comes in.

Here's what you'll learn in this chapter:

- What training is
- Why organizations need training
- What trainers do
- What qualities and characteristics a person needs to be a successful trainer

1. What *Is* Training?

According to human resources guru Dr. Leonard Nadler, "Training is learning that is provided in order to improve performance on the present job."

There are two implications in that statement. The first is that the current performance needs to be improved—there is a gap of some sort between what a person knows and is currently able to do and what the person needs to know and be able to do. The second is that the learning is not for some future use but is to be put to use immediately.

● ●

THINK ABOUT IT

Which of the following would you consider training?
- A. ___ A class in the basic principles of psychology.
- B. A tennis lesson.

(Continued)

C. A workshop on how to conduct hiring interviews.
D. A seminar in art history.
E. An online tutorial in using Excel.
F. On-the-job coaching in closing a sale.

●●●●●●●●●●●●●●●●●●●●●●●●●●●●●●●●●●●●●

You probably identified the tennis lesson (A), the workshop on conducting hiring interviews (C), the Excel tutorial (E), and the coaching for closing a sale (F) as training. Those experiences are intended to bring about an immediate change in the learner's performance. For example, people take tennis lessons because there is a gap between what they are able to do on the tennis court (get their serve in only once in a while) and what they want to be able to do (get their serve in more often). They attend an interviewing workshop because they need to close the gap between what they already know (how to be interviewed for a job) and what they need to know (how to interview someone else for a job).

Speaker, author, and master trainer Bob Pike says it succinctly at the opening of his book, *Creative Training Techniques:* "The purpose of any training program is to deliver results. People must be more effective after the training than they were before."

To put it another way, we might say that the purpose of training is to help people learn something they need to know or be able to do for a specific purpose—to achieve organizational objectives and goals, carry out specific tasks, prepare for new responsibilities, or attain their career goals. You might take an art history course for the pleasure of learning to look at art, or a class in the basic principles of psychology as the foundation for future learning. But you would probably take an Excel tutorial only if you needed to use the application to accomplish a specific goal, such as preparing a budget, and you would probably get coaching in closing a sale only if you needed those techniques to be better at your job.

When you think about it, you already know what training is—you've been through training, and you've been a trainer. Has someone taught you how to drive a car or plant a garden? You've been through training. Have you ever showed someone how to balance a checking account or prepare a holiday meal? You've been a trainer. Even though the subject matter and the learning methods differ widely, successful training programs share certain distinct characteristics:

- *They effect change.* They help people increase their knowledge, learn or improve their skills, or change their attitudes in order to change the current situation and achieve a desired outcome.

- *They are designed to achieve specific goals.* Those goals are the learning objectives that describe what people will be able to do as a result of training: "When learners complete this program, they will be able to [get their serve in 70 percent of the time] [conduct hiring interviews that meet legal requirements] [use Excel to prepare a budget] [ask questions to uncover a customer's needs]."

- *They are learner-centered, not trainer-centered.* The trainer's primary role is to be a guide for the learning process, not an expert who imparts information to passive learners.

- *They are designed to engage learners actively in the learning process.* The program uses interesting, relevant activities that help people discover new concepts, skills, and information and relate what they already know and have experienced.

- *They are relevant to the learners' real world.* The program focuses not on theory but on practical information, concepts and skills that learners can use immediately.

- *They have measurable outcomes.* The degree to which the program is successful in achieving the desired outcome can be observed or measured in some way.

2. Why Do Organizations Need Training?

All HR professionals must be prepared to get the most out of a workforce that is growing ever more diverse and to attract and retain the most highly skilled workers in an increasingly global knowledge and skills market.

Society for Human Resource Management (SHRM),
2006 Workplace Forecast

Training Fundamentals: Pfeiffer Essential Guides to Training Basics.
Copyright © 2010 by John Wiley & Sons, Inc.
Reproduced by permission of Pfeiffer, an Imprint of Wiley. www.Pfeiffer.com

Check What You Know

Why do you think organizations devote valuable resources to training? What do they get in return?

_____

_____

_____

_____

Training requires lots of resources—time, money, equipment, materials, facilities, expertise—that could be used for other purposes. Yet 62 percent of organizations surveyed in the 2006 Society for Human Resources Management Workplace Forecast reported that they were investing more in training and development. Even in tough economic times, although organizations may try to reduce costs by seeking more efficient ways to train employees, they continue to invest in training activities.

According to the 2006 Accenture Workplace survey, a company's workforce is increasingly important to business success. Training is essential for an organization to achieve its goals. Clerks in a retail store need to know how to process sales and treat customers in a way that makes them want to return. Airline mechanics need to know how to maintain and repair planes so they are safe to fly. Managers need to know how to give employees the clear expectations and feedback they need to be productive and help the organization achieve its strategic goals. Loan officers need to understand and follow ever-changing regulations. Even during belt-tightening times—_especially_ during such times, when there is no room for inefficiency and waste—training can significantly affect an organization's ability to succeed by helping people communicate more effectively, work more productively, and be more innovative.

Here's some of what training helps organizations do:

- _Develop and retain a leaner but more productive workforce._ Today's organizations are trying to compete and differentiate themselves in the marketplace by doing more with less. That means fewer, but more productive, employees. Improved performance improves productivity. It's that simple.

- *Keep up with the rapid pace of technological change.* Technology has changed the way we work, and the technology we use keeps changing—in fact, it often seems that just as we've mastered one software application or electronic device, another comes along and the learning process starts up again. No matter what the industry, people need ongoing training so they can make the best use of technology to help the organization stay competitive and achieve results.

- *Be more flexible.* We live in a rapidly changing world, and successful organizations are those that can respond quickly to changing situations. Organizations need to be flexible enough to respond to change quickly and effectively. Training that helps team members learn one another's jobs provides that kind of flexibility; so does training that helps improve employees' ability to be creative and innovative.

- *Understand cultural differences.* Today's companies need to find ways of being competitive in a global business environment. They also need to ensure high productivity among an increasingly diverse workforce. To accomplish those goals, they need to provide training that helps people understand and respect cultural differences and communicate effectively with people from diverse cultures.

- *Prepare new employees to do their jobs.* New employees at McDonald's and Starbucks go through training programs before they make their first hamburgers or caramel lattes. New bank tellers learn the bank's procedures before they handle customer transactions, and loan officers learn banking regulations before processing their first loan applications. In addition to sales skills, newly hired sales representatives need an in-depth understanding of the organizations' products. New employees in every industry need to learn their organizations' employee policies. Whether the training is done informally on the job, on a computer, or in a classroom, new employees need a significant amount of training just to get started. The better the initial training, the more rapidly the new person will become a productive member of the organization's workforce.

- *Prepare people to take on new responsibilities.* Once a new employee has settled into the job, the organization is likely to want that person to take on new responsibilities, perhaps even to move into another job. Just as training is essential for newly hired employees, training is needed to prepare people for new and different responsibilities so they can make a greater contribution to the organization's success.

Training Fundamentals: Pfeiffer Essential Guides to Training Basics.
Copyright © 2010 by John Wiley & Sons, Inc.
Reproduced by permission of Pfeiffer, an Imprint of Wiley. www.Pfeiffer.com

- *Attract and retain the best employees.* Organizations invest a great deal of money in hiring a new employee and preparing that person to be productive. To get a reasonable return on that investment, they need to find ways to encourage the best people to stay. Talented people have options about where they work, and today's workers expect opportunities to grow and develop. Organizations with good training and development programs are more attractive to job-seekers because they provide those opportunities. In fact, the availability of those programs can mean the difference between keeping or losing a good employee.

- *Comply with governmental requirements.* Many industries must comply with various federal, state, and local laws and government regulations. Many of those requirements are subject to frequent change, and companies can face serious consequences for failing to follow them. Thus, employees need ongoing or periodic training to make sure that they understand and abide by the laws and regulations that apply to the work they do.

- *Improve internal and external customer service.* Meeting customer needs is the reason that most organizations exist. The better able employees are to meet—and exceed—customers' expectations, the more successful the organization is likely to be. Employees need training that ensures they are able to provide their internal and external customers with excellent service.

- *Help organizations manage change.* Change is a fact of life—in fact, it is one of the few things we can all count on. At the same time, people tend to resist change and even to feel threatened by it. They often prefer to do things in familiar ways even when those ways are no longer productive; they might even continue to do things that no longer need to be done. Training can help people cope with change and provide new information and skills so that they can respond positively to changing situations and needs.

- *Improve and maintain quality.* Customers, whether internal or external, expect a certain level of quality from an organization's goods and services. Poor quality can have severe consequences—defective products can cause injuries; lack of attention to detail can lead to a botched surgical operation, a nuclear plant accident, or a banking crisis. Poor quality can cost companies a great deal of money—recalling products, correcting errors, losing customers. Organizations need ongoing training to keep the quality of goods and services at levels that keep people safe, keep costs under control, and maintain their competitive advantage.

3. What Do Trainers Do?

Check What You Know

The job description for the training position Justin is considering states that the successful candidate will be part of the team that provides training programs for all of the organization's employees. What tasks and responsibilities do you think that job description might include?

_____

_____

_____

_____

Some jobs seem relatively clear-cut: a mechanic fixes things, an engineer designs things, a sales representative sells things. You might think that the job of "trainer" falls into the same basket—trainers "train" or "teach" people to do things. That's true, as far as it goes. You could also say that trainers "help people learn what they need to know to perform their jobs in a way that helps the organization achieve its goals" or that they "help individuals develop their skills, increase their knowledge, and enhance their competencies." Still, even those broader descriptions of what trainers do only hint at the spectrum of responsibilities that trainers may have. Although teaching, or facilitating learning in a classroom, can be a significant part of a trainer's job, many trainers are involved in or responsible for other aspects of the training function as well. In fact, some people whose job title is "trainer" or "training specialist" never even set foot in a classroom.

The trainer's role differs widely from organization to organization, and often within organizations. Trainers' responsibilities depend on a whole range of situational factors, including the size of the organization, the type of industry, the organizational commitment to training, and where the responsibilities for meeting training needs lie. In a small company, the same person who handles hiring and employee benefits might be responsible for all the training, whereas large corporations usually have distinct departments that are devoted to training and employee development. In some organizations, trainers' responsibilities are limited to planning and delivering programs that are designed and developed by others; in others, the same people design, develop, and deliver training. Sometimes all an organization's training is delivered by internal trainers, who work for the company; in others, managers, subject-matter experts, and/or external consultants also deliver training.

When people first start out in the training field, chances are that they will be responsible for only a portion of their organization's training function. But since a trainer's responsibilities are likely to grow over time, it's important to understand all of the things that trainers do. Here's an overview:

- *Identify training needs and determine how to meet them.* All training programs start with a need, real or perceived. Trainers conduct needs assessments that help organizations determine which needs can be met by training and what type or types of training would be the most effective and efficient ways to meet specific needs.

- *Develop or find programs to meet specific training needs.* Trainers develop the learning objectives that form the foundation of a training program. They then design and develop—or find and adapt—training programs and materials that will help people achieve those objectives.

- *Deliver live training.* Trainers plan, prepare for, deliver, and follow up live, in-person workshops and virtual training programs.

- *Administer and support self-directed and on-the-job training.* A large percentage of training is being delivered on the job and in self-directed formats. Trainers help learners get started, provide guidance and support as they work, and track their progress.

- *Evaluate training success.* An important part of a trainer's job is to determine whether a training program achieved what it set out to achieve and identify changes that might be needed to improve it.

- *Make the business case for training.* To achieve their goals, organizations need continually to examine their activities to determine the real value of the investments they make, and training is no exception. Increasingly, trainers are called on to demonstrate the value of training to the organization's bottom line so that the organization knows whether its investment, including the time that people spend in training, is worthwhile.

4. What Makes a "Good" Trainer?

Keen listening and sensitive observational skills are two of the most essential attributes of a successful trainer.

in T.L. Gargiulo, A.M. Pangarkar, and T. Kirkwood (Eds.),
The Trainer's Portable Mentor "Introduction to Section Two"

Check What You Know

Suppose you were hiring a new trainer. Do either or both of the following candidates appear to be good candidates for the job? Why?

1. Danielle has a master's degree in journalism and an undergraduate degree in art history. For three years after college, she worked at a local museum setting up exhibits, planning events, leading tours, and writing a monthly newsletter. During college, she has spent several summers running art programs at a community center for which she also wrote several successful funding proposals. She enjoys playing chess and she coaches her son's soccer team.
   ❏ Good candidate? Why?

   _____

   _____

   _____

   _____

2. Jason graduated at the top of his university class with a B.S. in computer programming. After college, he worked as a website developer for a small consulting firm, where one of his sites won

   (Continued)

awards from a prestigious organization. For the past two years, he has been working on his own as a web designer and search optimization specialist for a variety of clients that include small businesses and nonprofit organizations. A competitive tennis player during college, he occasionally teaches tennis classes at a recreation center. Since high school, he has also done standup comedy for parties and clubs.

❏ Good candidate? Why?

_____

_____

_____

_____

Both Danielle and Jason possess several characteristics that would make them good candidates for a training position—but neither has all the characteristics that a trainer might need. That's because we're all better at some things than at others. Some of us are good at art, others at math. Some prefer to work with people, while others prefer working alone. Some are good at planning, others at execution. But like other professionals, the most successful trainers, and the ones who enjoy their work the most, have certain qualities and characteristics that have drawn them to the field. For example, every successful trainer I know communicates exceptionally well, sincerely likes working with people, and truly enjoys the process of learning.

THINK ABOUT IT

In addition to communicating clearly, working well with people, and enjoying the learning process, what other qualities and characteristics does a trainer need to be successful?

_____

_____

_____

_____

I've never met a trainer who exemplified all the qualities and characteristics in the list below. But successful trainers possess most of them to some degree, and they work diligently to improve or compensate for what they consider to be their more challenging areas.

- *Good communication skills.* The essence of a trainer's job is to get information across to others in a way that helps them learn. That means being able to communicate verbally, nonverbally, and in writing. Training professionals need to be able to convey information clearly and concisely—and they need to know how to listen. They need to know when to speak, and when to remain silent, how to encourage others to speak, and how to end a discussion. They need to know when and how to ask questions. Communication skills can be learned and improved, but because communicating is so vital to a trainer's job, the most successful training professional are people who truly enjoy communicating.

- *Enthusiasm for learning.* Scratch a trainer, and you'll usually find someone who loves to learn. That's good, because trainers are in a constant learning mode. Every new project brings a new challenge and a new learning curve. For most trainers, part of the fun is learning about subjects they would never have understood if they had not needed to teach them. In addition, trainers are continually challenged to learn more about the complex, rapidly changing field of training and to find ways in which they can improve their professional skills.

- *Creativity.* Training solutions are seldom simple. Trainers must consider a variety of factors—including limited resources—when deciding how to meet a specific need, and what works for one project might not work for the next. The most successful trainers are those who think creatively so they can go beyond obvious solutions and find innovative, cost-effective ways to help people learn.

- *Flexibility and the ability to think on one's feet.* People who like things to be pretty much the same day after day may find training a difficult field. Trainers need to be able and willing to change direction on a dime and respond quickly to the unexpected. The most successful trainers are those who can let go of what's not working, adapt quickly to change or new information, and deal with the challenges that are likely to come up just as they think that everything is under control.

*Training is a profession. It requires constant energy output.
If you tire quickly, become discouraged easily, or become
frustrated if things do not go according to plan, training may
not be for you.*

Elaine Biech,
Training for Dummies

- *Energy and enthusiasm.* Training is not a passive sport. It requires the active involvement and attention to detail that comes from being interested in what you do and caring about doing it well. Trainers who bring a contagious energy and enthusiasm to their work energize learners and stakeholders alike.

- *Good organizational, resource-management, and time-management skills.* Training is a constant juggling act—training professionals need to keep lots of balls in the air at the same time if they want to achieve results. Like any other project, training requires the ability to plan, stay on track and help others do the same; find and use resources; and make the most productive use of available time.

Training Fundamentals: Pfeiffer Essential Guides to Training Basics.
Copyright © 2010 by John Wiley & Sons, Inc.
Reproduced by permission of Pfeiffer, an Imprint of Wiley. www.Pfeiffer.com

- *The ability to work well with others.* Just as staging a theatrical production, putting on a conference, or getting a new product to market requires the collaborative efforts of a group, training is a team activity. Successful trainers don't hide away in cubicles; they engage with others to share ideas and solve problems so that the training programs they provide meet participants' needs and the organization's goals.

- *Good research, analytical, and problem-solving skills.* Someone once told me that training reminds them of putting together a puzzle without a picture. I agree—and that's one of the things I like about it. Most trainers, in fact, enjoy the challenges involved in figuring out how the puzzle goes together

---

ASTD Competency Study

The American Society for Training and Development (ASTD) has conducted extensive research into the roles, functions, and characteristics of people in the training field. ASTD's 2004 Competency Model for Learning and Performance describes three categories of foundational competencies—skills, knowledge, abilities, and behaviors—that a successful training professional needs to have or to develop. Those categories are interpersonal, business/management, and personal.

Interpersonal—Be able to build trust when interacting with others; communicate effectively; influence stakeholders and gain their commitment; leverage diversity and work well with diverse individuals; and network and partner to establish collaborative relationships

Business and management—Be able to analyze needs and propose solutions; apply business skills to understand business goals and build the case for investments in learning; drive results by identifying and achieving goals; plan and implement assignments; and think strategically.

Personal—Be able to demonstrate adaptability in the face of change and model personal development by continuing to learn and grow as a training professional,

For more information on this model and ASTD's other research in the training and development field, visit www.astd.org.

Training Fundamentals: Pfeiffer Essential Guides to Training Basics.
Copyright © 2010 by John Wiley & Sons, Inc.
Reproduced by permission of Pfeiffer, an Imprint of Wiley. www.Pfeiffer.com

Characteristics of Successful Trainers

- The ability to communicate verbally, nonverbally, and in writing
- An enthusiasm for learning
- The ability to think creatively
- Flexibility and ability to think on one's feet
- Energy and enthusiasm for what they are doing
- Good organizational, resource-management, and time-management skills
- The ability to work well with others
- Good research, analytical, and problem-solving skills
- Good people skills
- An enthusiasm for challenge
- Patience
- A good sense of humor

and find satisfaction in the process of seeking information, putting the pieces together, and coming up with the right solutions.

Good people skills. Trainers work with people and for people—and a great variety of people, at that. Those who are drawn to training as a career usually enjoy being with people, are able to listen well, can easily establish rapport, are able to empathize, can see things from other people's points of view, and are able to appreciate and respect people's differences.

Enthusiasm for challenge. Training is not for the faint of heart. Every day in a trainer's life brings new challenges, many of them completely unexpected. Instead of seeing challenges as something to be avoided, successful trainers welcome them as learning opportunities.

Patience. Things are not accomplished overnight in the training world (nor, usually, in any other world). Some things just take time, and impatience can easily lead to oversights and mistakes that can doom a training program. Trainers need the ability to be patient with themselves, as well as with others and with the vagaries of the situation.

- *Good sense of humor*. Trainers don't have to be comedians, or even to be able to pull off a joke (I'm not very good at that myself). But the ability to lighten up tense or difficult situations by being able to laugh at themselves and with others can be a valuable attribute for trainers. At the same time, trainers need to be able to recognize when humor, or specific kinds of humor, are out of place.

Quick Quiz

List the three to five key learning points from this chapter that will be most helpful to you.

_____

_____

_____

_____

_____

Training Fundamentals: Pfeiffer Essential Guides to Training Basics.
Copyright © 2010 by John Wiley & Sons, Inc.
Reproduced by permission of Pfeiffer, an Imprint of Wiley. www.Pfeiffer.com

What's Next?

A training professional's primary responsibility is to help people learn. That requires an understanding of the ways in which they learn, the differences between different types of learners, and the differences between different types of learning. That's what you'll find in the next chapter.

Apply What You Learned

Is training right for you? What are your strengths and challenges? On the assessment on pages 20 and 21, circle the number in the right-hand column to indicate how you rate yourself on each item. Then use the space below to summarize your responses to the rating. Think about these questions:

- Did anything surprise you? What?

_____

_____

_____

- What are strengths do you bring to the training field?

_____

_____

_____

- What are your biggest challenges? If you were to start a development plan today, where would you focus?

_____

_____

_____

Answers to Exercise

THINK ABOUT IT

Which of the following would you consider training?

A. ___ A class in the basic principles of psychology.
B. _X_ A tennis lesson.
C. _X_ A workshop on how to conduct hiring interviews.
D. ___ A seminar in art history.
E. _X_ An online tutorial in using Excel.
F. _X_ On-the-job coaching in closing a sale.

Training Fundamentals: Pfeiffer Essential Guides to Training Basics.
Copyright © 2010 by John Wiley & Sons, Inc.
Reproduced by permission of Pfeiffer, an Imprint of Wiley. www.Pfeiffer.com

Self-Assessment

Quality, Characteristic, or Skill

1. I am a good communicator.

2. I have enthusiasm for learning.

3. I am creative.

4. I am flexible and able to think on my feet.

5. I am energetic and enthusiastic about training.

6. I have good organizational, resource management, and time-management skills.

7. I work well with others.

8. I have good research, analytical, and problem-solving skills.

9. I have good people skills.

10. I enjoy challenges.

11. I can be patient.

12. I have a good sense of humor.

Worksheet

Excellent				Acceptable				Need to Improve	
1	2	3	4	5	6	7	8	9	10
1	2	3	4	5	6	7	8	9	10
1	2	3	4	5	6	7	8	9	10
1	2	3	4	5	6	7	8	9	10
1	2	3	4	5	6	7	8	9	10
1	2	3	4	5	6	7	8	9	10
1	2	3	4	5	6	7	8	9	10
1	2	3	4	5	6	7	8	9	10
1	2	3	4	5	6	7	8	9	10
1	2	3	4	5	6	7	8	9	10
1	2	3	4	5	6	7	8	9	10
1	2	3	4	5	6	7	8	9	10

Training Fundamentals: Pfeiffer Essential Guides to Training Basics.
Copyright © 2010 by John Wiley & Sons, Inc.
Reproduced by permission of Pfeiffer, an Imprint of Wiley. www.Pfeiffer.com

2

What to Know About Teaching Adults

Check What You Know

Justin decided to take advantage of the opportunity to become a trainer and is now a part of the Learning and Human Performance team. He was excited about conducting his first training program in his new position—an introduction to the government regulations that affect actions and decisions relating to employees for a group of twenty-five new supervisors. He had studied the topic in depth and came prepared with copious notes so that he could explain each of the regulations in detail. At the end of the two-hour session, he gave participants a chance to ask questions, although to his surprise, few of them did. Then, to check their understanding of the material he had covered, he gave them a short test, which he asked them to hand in on their way out the door along with an evaluation of the workshop.

Justin was surprised and dismayed by the results of both the test and the evaluation. The supervisors missed many of the items on the test. It was as if they had not even heard what he said. Worse, they rated the workshop "below average" on usefulness of the content and the trainer's presentation.

(Continued)

One supervisor, in fact, commented that the workshop was "boring" and a "waste of my valuable time."

What do you think went wrong? What could Justin have done differently to make the training program more successful?

_____

_____

_____

_____

As children, we went to school because that's what children do: our job was to pay attention and follow directions. Whether we loved school or hated it, whether our teachers helped us learn or bored us silly, we went. The powers that be—teachers, school boards, our parents—had decided that we should learn long division, geography, and Shakespeare, and so we did.

But that changed when we because adults. Learning is no longer our primary job. When we take time out of our busy schedules to learn something, it's because of reasons of our own. Maybe we have a passionate interest in art or music or gardening. Maybe we want to learn golf or tennis or carpentry. Maybe we want to take on more challenging responsibilities, get a promotion, make more money, pursue a new job opportunity, or embark on a new career. Whatever we decide to learn, we are no longer motivated primarily by what others expect from us but by what we want for ourselves.

Here's what's in this chapter:

- An overview of how adults learn
- Learner-centered versus trainer-centered training
- What differences in learning styles, preferences, and types of learning mean for trainers

Training Fundamentals: Pfeiffer Essential Guides to Training Basics.
Copyright © 2010 by John Wiley & Sons, Inc.
Reproduced by permission of Pfeiffer, an Imprint of Wiley. www.Pfeiffer.com

1. How Adults Learn

Understanding how adults learn helps us design, develop, and deliver training programs that achieves their intended results. If we want people to learn, our programs must be learner-centered instead of teacher-centered.

Maryellen Weimer,
Learner-Centered Teaching

● ●

THINK ABOUT IT

Imagine that you are about to participate in a workshop to learn how to give a presentation. Which of the following instructional approaches would be most likely to help you learn?

1. The trainer, Sam, opens the workshop by asking participants to introduce themselves. He reviews the workshop objectives and agenda and hands out copies of his PowerPoint slides, which, he tells participants, "You can use to take notes." He presents information about several topics: the criteria for an effective presentation, the process of planning and preparing for a presentation, guidelines for presenting effectively, and presentation techniques. At the end of each topic, he reviews the key learning points and gives participants a chance to ask questions. Before explaining the presentation techniques, he shows a funny fifteen-minute film on presentation skills. When the film is over, he reviews a slide with the key points. At the end of the workshop, participants take a test to see how well they remember what the trainer said.

(Continued)

2. After asking participants to think about how learning to make better presentations will benefit them, the trainer, Juanita, asks them to think of some presentations they gave or attended. Working in small groups, they discuss what makes a presentation work. Each group then develops a worksheet for planning a presentation and a set of guidelines for delivering a presentation. After each group discussion, the groups summarize their key points for the entire group or write those points on flip-chart pages that are posted on the walls so everyone can walk around and read them. The trainer shows a funny film on presentation skills and then asks participants questions about how what they saw relates to their earlier discussions. Each group then works together to plan and deliver a brief presentation for the whole group. At the end of the workshop, participants assess their strengths and challenges and make an action plan for applying what they learned to improve their presentations.

Which instructional approach would be most likely to help you learn? Why?

☐ Sam's   ☐ Juanita's

_____

_____

_____

_____

• •

Most people would say that Juanita's approach describes the way they would learn best. In Sam's workshop, as in Justin's, the learners are passive—all they are expected to do is listen, take notes, and ask questions. Even if they were able to answer all the questions on the test, chances are that no real learning would have taken place. They will not necessarily leave the workshop with a change in their performance; in this case, an improved ability to plan, prepare for, and deliver effective presentations.

Training Fundamentals: Pfeiffer Essential Guides to Training Basics.
Copyright © 2010 by John Wiley & Sons, Inc.
Reproduced by permission of Pfeiffer, an Imprint of Wiley. www.Pfeiffer.com

In Juanita's workshop, however, the learners are actively involved right from the beginning. She helps them draw on their own experience and knowledge and relate what they already know to the topic at hand. She provides activities that help them discover new strategies and ideas, gives them opportunities to practice what they are learning, and helps them think about how to apply what they learn after the workshop is over.

Juanita understands the key principles of adult learning: adults need to be engaged and involved, see how the learning will benefit them, and be able to relate what they are learning to what they already know.

Treat adult learners as if they have little or no experience when they do, and you insult them and lose them. It is critical to effective training that you acknowledge the rich store of experience your learners possess . . . and exploit it. Help them to contribute to their own and other people's learning.

Harold D. Stolovitch and Erica J. Keeps,
Telling Ain't Training

Many people have done extensive research into the ways that adults learn. But much of what we know can be traced back to the work of adult learning expert Malcolm Knowles, who identified a number of characteristics of adult learners that form the underpinnings of today's successful educational and training programs. In essence, those characteristics are that adults:

- Are independent and self-directed
- Bring all their experiences, knowledge, and priorities to training
- Want to know why they are learning
- Respond primarily to internal, rather than external, motivators

Let's look each of those characteristics more closely.

Adults are independent and self-directed. As adults, we are do not like to see ourselves as passive creatures who go where we are told and let learning "happen" to us. Instead, we want opportunities to make our own decisions and take responsibility for our own learning. We not only want to decide what we are going to learn, but we want to be actively involved in the learning process. We want to be treated as—well, as adults.

Adults bring all their experience, knowledge, and priorities to training. Adult learners are not blank slates—far from it. We bring with us everything we already know, the experiences we've had in our personal lives and our careers, our beliefs and biases, and our points of view and attitudes, all of which form the foundation for new learning (and which can also create resistance to the learning process). Our experience can be a valuable resource for us and for our fellow learners. But for us to learn and to retain what we learn, we need opportunities to make connections between what we are learning and what we already know.

The learning process can be difficult for some people, and some adults can be reluctant to learn because they lack confidence. Wellesley Foshay, Kenneth Silber, and Michael Stelnicki, the authors of *Writing Training Materials That Work*, use the acronym "YCDI," which stands for "You can do it." They explain that "People are more likely to learn when they feel that they are mastering the new knowledge. To build confidence, relate the ways in which other learners have succeeded or explain how the people who are taking this training have already acquired knowledge related to the present content." (See the table on the next page.)

Adults want to know why they are learning. Training is not learning for learning's sake. We adults need to know why we need to learn and how what we learn will benefit us. We expect to be able to use what we learn, need to see the relevance to our goals, and understand how to apply the learning in the real world. There's a commonly used acronym for this concept: "WIIFM," which means, "What's in it for me?" The more successful a training program is at helping learners answer that question, the more likely it is that they will become engaged and actively involved in the learning process.

Adults respond primarily to internal motivators. As mentioned in Chapter 1, we adults attend classes, take lessons, and participate in training because there is something we want. We usually respond less to external motivators such as promises of rewards or threats of punishment than to internal motivators: greater self-esteem, more confidence, increased recognition, a sense of belonging, the satisfaction of meeting challenges, a sense of self-fulfillment. It is important to us that our experience and knowledge are valued. We respond best when we are seen as equals in the training environment.

Key Differences Between Child and Adult Learners

Children	Adults
Let others tell them what they are supposed to learn	Want to decide for themselves what they are going to learn
Accept what they are told	Examine what they are told in terms of their experiences, beliefs, and values
Expect to use what they learn sometime in the future	Expect to put the learning to use right away
Have little or no prior knowledge and experience to which new learning can be connected	Have a lot of prior knowledge and experience to which new learning can be connected
Are open to new learning	May have biases and fixed ideas that cause resistance to learning

2. What Is Learner-Centered Training?

THINK ABOUT IT

Which of the following best describes a typical day in the various classes and workshops you have attended since you have become an adult (including college)?

____1. The teacher, instructor, or trainer stood in front of the group, gave a lecture, and handed out an assignment.

____2. The teacher, instructor, or trainer posed a problem for the members of the group to solve and/or facilitated a discussion on the topic.

It would not be surprising if you checked the first example. That statement describes a traditional teacher-centered classroom, where the teacher (or trainer) is the most important person, whose role is to impart knowledge to people who know little or nothing about the subject. We're all more than familiar with this approach to teaching. Teaching and learning expert Maryellen Weimer reports that a university research study found that almost half of the faculty used lecture as their primary method of instruction, even when they incorporated some discussion and other activities into their classes.

The traditional teacher-centered approach is not limited to college classrooms; it's an approach that is still all-too common in training. After all, if the goal is to get information across, shouldn't the focus be on delivering that information and hammering it in so that people remember it? And what easier, quicker way is there to deliver content than to give a lecture (or a presentation, which is essentially the same thing), and then give learners a test to make sure that they were paying attention.

But wait . . . isn't the goal of training to help people learn so that they can use the learning *to do something?* If you sat and listened while someone told you how to set up a bookkeeping system for your personal finances, it's unlikely that you could go right home and do the job. Sitting through a presentation on team leadership would hardly prepare you to lead a team, nor would listening to someone talk about how to give a presentation do much to help you learn how to give one yourself. In all three cases, you would probably pick up useful tips, but you would not have *learned* much that you could put to immediate use.

The second example, where the teacher, instructor, or trainer posed a problem for the group to solve and/or facilitated a discussion, describes a learning experience that is more *learner-centered*: The most important people are the learners, and the role of the teacher, or trainer, is to help them learn. Lecture might be one of the methods, but it's only one of many, and its use is limited to providing content people need so that they can *do* something.

Learner-centered teachers are guides, facilitators, and designers of the learning experience. They are no longer the main performer, the one with the most lines, or the one working harder than everyone else. . . . The action in the learner-centered classroom features the students.

Maryellen Weimer,
Learner-Centered Teaching

Training Fundamentals: Pfeiffer Essential Guides to Training Basics.
Copyright © 2010 by John Wiley & Sons, Inc.
Reproduced by permission of Pfeiffer, an Imprint of Wiley. www.Pfeiffer.com

How Trainers Use a Learner-Centered Approach

What trainers sometimes do not realize is that they are not responsible for participants' learning. Participants are responsible for their own learning. The trainer is a guide who is responsible for creating and maintaining an environment in which people are able to learn.

In a teacher-centered classroom, some students are likely to learn well because they know how to do something with the information they receive. Many, however, leave the class or the workshop with only a vague idea about how to use what they have learned. A learner-centered approach is one of the key criteria that distinguishes successful training programs—those that result in an actual change in participants' behavior and provide skills and knowledge they can apply to their real world.

Andragogy and Pedagogy

If you do any reading about theories of how people learn, you are likely to run across these two terms. "Andragogy," which was coined by a German teacher nearly two centuries ago, is most often associated with Dr. Malcolm Knowles, widely accepted as a central figure in the field of adult education. Andragogy describes an approach to learning that is focused on the learners, not on the teacher—a polar opposite of the traditional pedagogical model in which the teacher is the expert and the learners passive recipients of his or her knowledge.

How long can you sit and listen to a fact-based lecture, devoid of stories, emotion, or anything that connects you personally to the content? Your tolerance for such a learning experience is probably minimal, and the actual time you can remain sitting without getting fidgety is probably a matter of minutes, not hours.

Sharon Bowman,
Training from the Back of the Room

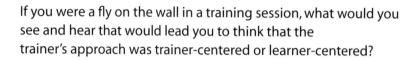

THINK ABOUT IT

If you were a fly on the wall in a training session, what would you see and hear that would lead you to think that the trainer's approach was trainer-centered or learner-centered?

Trainer-Centered	Learner-Centered

Here's what you might see in the trainer-centered session: Participants would be seated so that they all faced the trainer, who would be standing in front of the group talking, perhaps showing a series of slides and using a laser pointer to call the group's attention to specific points. The participants might or might not be taking notes. If they were highly motivated to learn about the subject and the trainer had an engaging style, they might be sitting slightly forward in their seats, their eyes focused on the trainer and the slides. If they were not highly motivated, and if the trainer did not have an engaging style, they might be slumped in their chairs, and some might actually be dozing.

Here's what the learner-centered session might look like: Participants would be seated in small groups at separate tables arranged so that they could see the trainer and one another. If the trainer is speaking, he or she would be asking lots of questions. Participants might be holding discussions in small groups or practicing something they had learned while the trainer moved around to answer questions or give them feedback. There would be a lot of energy in the room; everyone would be engaged and involved in his or her own way.

When trainers keep the learners' needs front and center, they do the following:

- *Create a safe, supportive environment that is conducive to learning.* Have you ever watched a small child learn to put differently shaped blocks into matching holes in a plastic ball? She experiments: she tries to put a square block into a round hole or a diamond-shaped block into a square hole, a round block into a cross-shaped hole, again and again. Mommy and Daddy show her how it's done and provide words of encouragement: "That's good, honey, try again, you're almost there." Suddenly, a block matches up with the right hole and drops inside the ball. Mommy and Daddy clap with delight. The toddler gets the idea that success is possible—and that it is rewarding. She keeps on trying, and soon it become easier to get the right blocks in the right holes. The child has learned to do something, not by being told how to do it, but by trying it out, making mistakes, getting feedback, and trying again.

  Adults also learn by trying things out, making mistakes, and trying again. They also need words of encouragement and feedback that let them know what's working and what they need to do differently. They need an environment in which they can feel comfortable experimenting, taking risks, and learning from their mistakes.

- *Understand and respect learners' diverse needs and learning styles.* We like to learn in different ways. Some of us prefer to learn by watching and listening; others by talking; others by touching and moving. Some of us process information more quickly than others. Some of us love to work in groups; others prefer to work on their own. As trainers, we need to understand and respect these kinds of differences and use a variety of approaches to meet different needs and styles. (There is more about learning styles later in this chapter.)

- *Focus on relevant outcomes.* In ancient Rome, the tall obelisks in front of churches, which could be seen from miles away, alerted pilgrims to their destination. Having a clear destination kept them on the right path and told them when they had arrived. But for adult learners, knowing the outcome of training isn't enough. To stay engaged, they need to see the relevance of what they are learning—how it will benefit them and their organization.

- *Make training active.* Everyone learns more when he or she is actively engaged and involved in the learning process. That means far less talking on the part of the trainer and far more on the part of the learners. It means that, instead of telling people things, learner-centered trainers ask lots and lots of questions that get people thinking about the subject and relating it to what they already know. It means providing activities that help people learn through discovery, discussion, analysis, collaboration, experimentation, and practice. (You'll learn more about training activities in Chapter 5.)

- *Provide feedback and positive reinforcement.* If you've ever tried to learn a sport—to play tennis or golf, for example—you know that you feel like a complete klutz when you first begin. You don't know how to stand, to move, to hold the racquet or the club. You swing and miss the ball, again and again. It can be very discouraging. Comments such as, "No, not like that" or "That's wrong" don't help much. Useful feedback that tells you what you need to do differently—"a little lower," "a little faster," "step back," "step forward," "keep your eye on the ball"—lets you make the adjustments needed for small successes. And positive reinforcement—"That's right! Good work"—when you master any small part of the process keeps you going. It's the same with anything that we learn. We need feedback and positive reinforcement to get through the confusion, lack of understanding, and klutziness that is part of the learning process.

- *Help people apply the learning to real-world situations.* Adults want to be able to use what they learn, and they learn best by doing. Suppose you decided to take a course in interior design. No matter how enjoyable the course, you would want to walk away with new knowledge and skills that you could use to redecorate your home or start a new career. You'd learn more if you had opportunities to apply what you learned to real design projects during the course and get feedback on your work from the instructor and the other students. (You might even walk out with a portfolio to show prospective clients.) Teachers and trainers need constantly to seek ways to help people relate what they are learning—and, to the extent possible, to apply it to real situations.

How Trainers Use a Learner-Centered Approach

- Create an environment that is conducive to learning, where people can try things out, make mistakes, get feedback, and try again.
- Understand and respect learners' diverse needs and learning styles.
- Focus on relevant outcomes and help people see how learning will benefit them.
- Make training active – help participants become actively engaged and involved in the learning process.
- Provide feedback and positive reinforcement.
- Help people apply the learning to real-world situations.

THINK ABOUT IT

Think about something you learned recently in your personal or professional life (not at school). Would you describe the class, workshop, or learning program as learner-centered? Why or why not?

_____

_____

_____

_____

What could have the trainer or program designer done to make it easier for you to learn?

_____

_____

_____

_____

Training Fundamentals: Pfeiffer Essential Guides to Training Basics.
Copyright © 2010 by John Wiley & Sons, Inc.
Reproduced by permission of Pfeiffer, an Imprint of Wiley. www.Pfeiffer.com

3. Differences in Learning Styles and Preferences

• •

THINK ABOUT IT

We all like to learn in different ways. What are your learning preferences? Which of the activities in this list describe the ways in which you like to learn?

- ❏ Sharing ideas and working on projects with others
- ❏ Analyzing situations and solving problems
- ❏ Having Hands-on experiences in real or realistic situations
- ❏ Completing exercises in an e-learning program
- ❏ Participating in group discussions
- ❏ Listening to stories
- ❏ Responding to discussion questions
- ❏ Working on my own to answer questions in a workbook
- ❏ Listening to a presentation or a lecture
- ❏ Participating in role plays and simulations
- ❏ Sharing my ideas and opinions with a group
- ❏ Sharing my feelings with others
- ❏ Brainstorming activities
- ❏ Looking at information that is presented visually (slides, flip charts, posters, flow charts)
- ❏ Working one-on-one with a coach or mentor
- ❏ Activities that involve reading and/or writing

• •

When I'm shopping for clothes and see "one size fits all" on a label, I usually sigh and put the garment back on the rack. I'm on the "petite" end of the size spectrum, and one-size-fits-all clothing is much too big for me. What the maker really should have said is, "One size fits all average-sized people."

In terms of training, one size also does not fit all. We have different ways of processing information, different ways of receiving information, and different learning preferences. For example, I learn well by talking things through and by trying things out for myself. When I attend a presentation, I retain more of what people say when it is reinforced by visuals; I also learn well by making notes while I read or listen to a speaker. On the other hand, one of my close colleagues tends to sit and listen quietly during meetings and workshops, seldom venturing an opinion, writing anything down, or asking a question. Yet when the event is over, she usually remembers with great clarity nearly everything she heard.

An understanding of the different ways in which people receive and process information helps trainers figure out the best instructional methods, activities, and media to help everyone to learn. And recognizing that not everyone learns in the same way that we do allows us to be more flexible and responsive to our learners' needs.

There is a great deal of literature available on learning styles and preferences, and a certain amount of controversy about the various theories. Learning is a very complex process, one that is still not fully understood, and no one model or theory completely explains how we learn. But an understanding of the different theories and models can increase your ability to identify the best approach in a given situation, and recognizing that not everyone learns in the same way that we do allows us to be more flexible and responsive to our learners' needs. Below, I've tried to distill some of the key information into a "user-friendly" form that I hope will give you the basics. When you're ready to learn more, you can consult some in the books in the Resources, or just put "adult learning styles" into a search engine and you'll find a wealth of resources. In the meantime, use this information with the understanding that people are never easily categorized and that everyone has more than one way of learning.

Four Primary Learning Styles or Preferences

Peter Honey and Alan Mumford's Learning Styles Questionnaire, which is based on psychologist David Kolb's learning styles model, identifies four primary types of learners: Activists, Reflectors, Theorists, and Pragmatists.

- *Activists*, also described as "Doers," like to get their hands dirty. They enjoy the process of experimenting, exploring, and discovering. They tend to jump right into things without worrying about what might happen. In a meeting or workshop, they are the people who speak up most quickly (and most often) and eagerly volunteer to lead or participate in activities. Activists become restless when asked to sit for long periods listening or engaging in lengthy discussions. They are anxious to practice what they are learning and see how they can apply it in the real world.

- *Reflectors*, also described as "Reviewers" or "Observers," prefer to learn by watching and listening. They like to think about what they are going to say before they offer their opinions or conclusions, and they do not like to be pressured. It's easy for trainers to think that, because they do not speak up readily, they are not paying attention, but like my friend, reflectors can be as engaged—even more engaged—as activists like me who enthusiastically jump in to answer every question and take the lead role in discussions. In fact, when reflectors do speak up, their responses and comments tend to be accurate and insightful.

- *Theorists*, also described as "Thinkers," like to think things through, analyze them in a step-by-step way, and evaluate them, so they can come to logical conclusions. They like to discuss facts, theories, models, and systems and they can be uncomfortable or impatient with what they consider to be "touchy-feely" concepts and activities. They prefer a methodical approach, and they tend to ask a lot of questions, sometimes challenging the information, concepts, or processes that are being presented. They want clear goals and objectives, like to work independently, and may not see the point of role-playing exercises and simulations.

- *Pragmatists*, also described as "Planners," like to solve problems. They can become impatient with too much theory and lengthy discussions. They want to know how what they are learning applies to the "real" world, and they want to cut to the chase—to jump in and try it out themselves.

Three Primary Sensory Receivers

Research suggests that our learning preferences differ in the ways in which we rely on our senses to receive and process information. A well-known model postulates that we have three primary sensory receivers: Visual, Auditory, and Kinesthetic (VAK). Although we use all three when we learn, the theory is that one or two are usually more dominant, so training programs that combine different types of media, presentation methods, and activities are likely to increase learning and retention for greater numbers of people.

- *Visual learners:* Visual learners are those who like to have information presented through pictures, diagrams, demonstrations, and other visual media or through reading and writing. Being able to see the speaker along with visual examples such as flowcharts, bar graphs, pictures, outlines, or displays of key learning points that illustrate or reinforce the spoken words helps these learners follow and understand what they hear, and taking notes helps them fix what they hear in their minds. They tend to have good visual memories; for example, they might be able to read a map once and then remember whether to turn right or left at the intersection; they are better at remembering faces than names; and they can often visualize the page on a book in which certain information appears.

- *Auditory learners:* These learners take in information better through the ears than through the eyes, and they often remember more of what they hear than what they see. They listen well, but they also like to talk. They like verbal exchanges of ideas, stories, and anecdotes, and may use pneumonic devices to remember information. They may remember names but not faces and have difficulty following printed directions or diagrams. In training sessions, they prefer activities that involve listening and talking, such as lectures, brainstorming, and discussions.

- *Kinesthetic learners:* Many people learn best by moving and touching. They prefer trying something out rather than talking about it or watching a demonstration. They may become bored with too much discussion or talking and may stand up or move while a trainer is speaking. They like to take notes, draw pictures, or simply doodle when they are asked to listen, and they may lose focus when they need to sit still for too long. They prefer activities that get them up and moving and provide hands-on practice.

Multiple Intelligences

Another way to think about different learning styles is the model developed by Harvard Professor of Education Howard Gardner. Dr. Gardner postulated that each of us relies on one or two out of eight different "intelligences" or skills that we use to solve different kinds of problems. These intelligences are valued differently in different cultures. In the United States, for example, we tend to value verbal-linguistic and logical-mathematical intelligences over others, and those preferences are often reflected in our learning and educational systems.

Here is an overview of the eight "intelligences":

- *Verbal-Linguistic.* People who respond well to words—written and verbal communication—and learn well through activities that involve listening, speaking, reading, and word games.

- *Logical-mathematical.* People who are good at numbers and logic; they learn by organizing, outlining, calculating, and solving problems.

- *Musical.* People who are sensitive to rhythm, music, and lyrics, which can help them learn.

- *Spatial.* People who think and remember in pictures, often using symbols, doodles, diagrams, and mind-maps to learn.

- *Bodily-kinesthetic.* People who like physical activity, sports, games, drama, and dancing; they learn through doing, taking action, and writing notes, and they need frequent breaks when learning.

- *Interpersonal.* People who good with others and have a good understanding of relationships; they like learning from others and in teams, collaborating, and teaching.

- *Intrapersonal.* People who are comfortable with their own emotional lives; good at self-discovery, reflection, and concentration, they often like to work independently rather than with others.

- *Naturalist.* People who relate easily to the natural world and can often learn well from activities that involve the outdoors.

THINK ABOUT IT

How do you prefer to learn? Which of these descriptions fit you most closely?

- ❏ I like activities that involve listening, speaking, reading, and word games.
- ❏ I enjoy organizing, outlining, calculating, and solving problems.
- ❏ I am sensitive to rhythm, music, and lyrics.
- ❏ I like to use symbols, doodles, diagrams, and mind-maps when I learn.
- ❏ I enjoy physical activity, sports, games, drama, and dancing.
- ❏ I like learning from others and in teams, collaborating, and teaching.
- ❏ I am good at self-discovery, reflection, and concentration, and I prefer to work independently.
- ❏ I can often learn well from activities that involve the outdoors.

Check What You Know

Suppose you were designing a training program to teach new supervisors to give helpful feedback to their employees. What are some of the things you could include in the design to make sure that people with diverse learning styles and preferences would be able to learn?

_____

_____

_____

_____

_____

_____

_____

_____

_____

The challenge for those of us who design and deliver training is to come up with ways to meet our learners' diverse styles and needs. We do that by varying the ways in which we present information and the kinds of learning activities we use.

Just as carpenters need lots of different tools so they can do different types of jobs, trainers need a variety of tools so they can help different people learn the same information and skills in different ways. Here are some examples:

- Use printed information, diagrams, charts, and slides to accompany information that we present verbally.

- Provide handouts that are formatted to encourage note-taking.

- Mix up activities that involve listening and talking with experiential activities and hands-on practice.
- Present learners with problems to solve and cases to analyze.
- Provide opportunities for people to work on structured individual activities.
- Help people reflect quietly on what they are learning.
- Use videos and audiotapes, music, art, and games to provide variety and stimulate the senses.
- Get people on their feet after they have been sitting for a while.

4. Differences in Types of Learning

Check What You Know

Match the description to the type of learning.

Types of learning: (K) gain or improve knowledge; (S) gain or improve skills; or (A) change attitude

Description
1. _____ Learning to change a tire.
2. _____ Learning to identify the bones in the human body.
3. _____ Learning to respect differing points of view.
4. _____ Learning to work collaboratively with team members on projects.
5. _____ Learning to analyze a problem to discover its root cause.
6. _____ Learning to design a website.

In addition to differences in learning styles, there are differences in the types of learning. An understanding of the different types is important for a trainer to be able to develop learning objectives and select the best activities to help people learn.

Three Learning Domains

In the 1950s, Dr. Benjamin Bloom and his colleagues at the University of Chicago identified three primary categories, or domains, of learning (commonly referred to as "KSAs" or "Bloom's Taxonomy"): Knowledge, Skills, and Attitude.

- The *knowledge (cognitive) domain* refers to mental activity—the ability to acquire, understand, recall, evaluate, process, and use data and information. Teaching people to select the right tool for a job, follow a procedure, create a spreadsheet for comparing costs, follow the rules of a game, evaluate candidates for a position, speak a new language, design a website or an office layout, write a proposal, or analyze a problem would fall into this category.

- The *psychomotor (skills) domain* refers to physical movement, coordination, and motor skills— manual or physical skills that require practice to attain. This category includes the skills people need to be able to change a tire or operate a forklift, assemble or repair equipment, hit a softball, build an architectural model, prepare a meal, operate a retail checkout system, or play the violin.

> ## Declarative vs. Procedural Knowledge
>
> When you are looking for the best way to teach something, think about whether you want people to learn *about* it (declarative knowledge) or learn *how to do* it (procedural knowledge). Knowing the difference can help you select the right instructional methods and learning activities.
>
> - Declarative knowledge is facts, concepts, and principles: a set of rules for a baseball game, the characteristics of different automobiles, an organization's values statements.
> - Procedural knowledge is "how-to" knowledge: how to process a claim, cook a turkey, repair a broken pipe, write a marketing plan, prepare a spreadsheet.

- The *affective (attitude) domain* refers to emotions, feelings, values, and attitudes. Learning to treat others with respect, listen actively, present a professional image, work collaboratively with team members, behave in an ethical manner, or behave more responsibly fall into this category.

Training Fundamentals: Pfeiffer Essential Guides to Training Basics.
Copyright © 2010 by John Wiley & Sons, Inc.
Reproduced by permission of Pfeiffer, an Imprint of Wiley. www.Pfeiffer.com

What's Next?

The process of developing and delivering a training program can seem overwhelming. There is so much to consider, so many questions to ask, so many decisions to make, and so many tasks to carry out. In the next chapter, you'll learn about a tried-and-tested system that training professionals use to make sure that the training they provide meets real needs while making the best use of the organization's resources.

Apply What You Learn

Answer these questions about the training program that you have selected to work on while you are reading this book.

1. What will the program be intended to do? Provide or enhance knowledge? Provide or improve skills? Change attitudes? All three?

    _____

    _____

    _____

2. What are some ways in which you can make the program learner-centered, rather than trainer-centered?

    _____

    _____

    _____

    _____

    _____

3. What are some ways in which you can meet the needs of participants with different learning styles?

    _____

    _____

    _____

    _____

    _____

Answers to Exercise

Check What You Know

Match the description to the type of learning.

Types of learning: (K) gain or improve knowledge; (S) gain or improve skills; or (A) change attitude

Description

1. S   Learning to change a tire.
2. K   Learning to identify the bones in the human body.
3. A   Learning to respect differing points of view.
4. A   Learning to work collaboratively with team members on projects.
5. K   Learning to analyze a problem to discover its root cause.
6. K   Learning to design a website.

3

Designing Training Programs

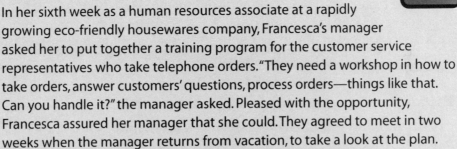

Check What You Know

In her sixth week as a human resources associate at a rapidly growing eco-friendly housewares company, Francesca's manager asked her to put together a training program for the customer service representatives who take telephone orders. "They need a workshop in how to take orders, answer customers' questions, process orders—things like that. Can you handle it?" the manager asked. Pleased with the opportunity, Francesca assured her manager that she could. They agreed to meet in two weeks when the manager returns from vacation, to take a look at the plan.

Although Francesca is delighted with this assignment, she isn't sure where to begin. She thinks about the workshops she attended at her last job, reads through the procedures in the new online customer service manual, and then starts to draw up an outline. But after working on the outline for two days, she realizes that she has too many unanswered questions to proceed. She wants to be ready with a plan when her manager returns, but she suspects that she is in deep water, and it's about to go over her head. Not knowing what else to do, she sends an e-mail to a colleague who has been working in the training field for several years and asks for help.

Francesca's colleague gets back to her right away, saying that he'll be glad to help. What are some of the suggestions he might have made about the steps she needs to take to come up with a plan for this training?

_____

_____

_____

When our children were small, my husband and I decided to renovate our home, a hillside house that had been built in the 1920s as a summer cottage. We had a somewhat vague goal—we just wanted the place to be more livable. In an attempt to keep costs within our mostly nonexistent budget, we chose not to consult with an architect or even to hire a licensed contractor; instead, we gave the job to a carpenter who had been recommended by friends.

I'm sure you've guessed that the project was a nightmare. The carpenter ran into problem after problem all along the way. Even though we achieved some of our goals, the haphazard renovation cost us far more than we'd planned to spend with less than satisfactory results. But it was definitely a learning experience. Among other things, I learned that projects like remodeling a home—and designing a training program—do not just happen. To achieve the results you want within the budget you have, it's essential to have both clear objectives and a realistic plan for achieving them. And the more attention you pay to the planning process, the more likely your project is to get results.

In this chapter we'll cover:

- The purpose of the instructional design process
- ADDIE, the most commonly used system for designing a training program
- What's involved in analyzing the need for training
- Writing the learning objectives that form the foundation for any training program

An educational [or training] need is most often defined as a discrepancy or gap between what presently is and what should be. . . . This "what should be" is described in a number of ways—as desired results, future states or conditions, changes in performance, or expected outcomes.

Rosemary Caffarella,
Planning Programs for Adult Learners, p. 114

1. Purpose of the Instructional Design Process

Check What You Know

1. Where does the idea that training is needed come from?

    _____

    _____

    _____

    _____

2. What are some of the reasons that people in organizations request training?

    _____

    _____

    _____

    _____

3. Does a request for training mean that training is necessarily needed? Why or why not?

    _____

    _____

    _____

    _____

Training programs begin with an idea that something needs to change. The idea can come from almost anyone in an organization—an executive who thinks that team leaders are holding too many useless meetings; a product support team that is preparing for the introduction of a new product; a quality control manager who has received a mandate to reduce product defects; supervisors who want to make sure that employees comply with new government regulations; a manager whose salespeople have failed to meet targets; or an executive team that is looking for ways to retain valuable employees and make them more productive. People commonly request training when new change initiatives, systems, regulations, procedures, policies, products, or services are introduced or when there is a reorganization of some kind. They also think of training when individuals or teams fail to meet performance targets, morale is low, customer complaints or accidents are on the rise, deadlines are frequently missed, or other problems impact the organization's ability to achieve its goals.

But the idea that training is needed doesn't necessarily mean that training *is* needed. In fact, organizations often waste time and money developing and delivering training programs when there are other, less expensive and time-consuming (and possibly, more effective) ways to effect change, and when changing the situation is not necessary for the organization to achieve its goals. And even when training is the answer, they may buy a Mercedes when a Vespa would do.

To avoid wasting resources on training that doesn't do the job, is unnecessary, or costs too much, the people responsible for designing and developing training programs need a logical, practical, realistic process for making sure that the training is relevant, cost-effective, and likely to achieve the intended results. For many training professionals, that process is some form of the model commonly known as ADDIE. Although there are other approaches to instructional design, most instructional designers would agree that ADDIE has both the structure and the flexibility to keep them on the right track.

2. All About ADDIE

As you may have guessed, ADDIE is an acronym for the key steps in the process: Analysis, Design, Development, Implementation, and Evaluation.

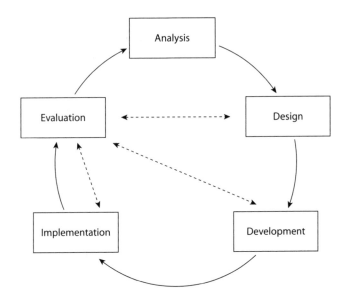

The ADDIE Model

ADDIE, which has its basis in an instructional systems approach to solving training problems established by the U.S. Department of Defense, provides a structured approach to the essential tasks and decisions in the instructional design process. Although we'll talk about the steps in a linear way, ADDIE is not necessarily a linear process; instead, it's dynamic and interactive, with evaluation and feedback at every step of the way. For a given project, you might not follow the steps in order, you might skip some steps, and you will often return to earlier steps in light of new information. When using this (or any other) instructional design process, it's important to keep an open mind and be willing to rethink your original ideas and perceptions in the light of new information.

The ADDIE process can be used to design an organization's entire training program, identify and meet the training needs of a unit within the organization, or address one training request. For purposes of this book, we will look at how ADDIE is used to design and develop a program to meet one training need.

Below is an overview of the process. You'll learn more about the five stages in the rest of this chapter and in Chapters 4, 5, and 6 of this book.

The Stages of the ADDIE Process

Check What You Know

What do you think is involved in each stage of the ADDIE instructional design process? For each of the five stages, briefly describe the purpose and what takes place:

ANALYSIS
- Purpose: _____
- What takes place: _____
  _____
  _____

DESIGN
- Purpose: _____
- What takes place: _____
  _____
  _____

DEVELOPMENT
- Purpose: _____
- What takes place: _____
  _____
  _____

IMPLEMENTATION
- Purpose: _____

- **What takes place:** _____

_____

_____

EVALUATION
- **Purpose:** _____
- **What takes place:** _____

_____

_____

In the analysis stage, instructional designers can never know too much. Curiosity is the first analysis skill that belongs in a designer's tool kit, where it will pay countless dividends. It is impossible to ask too many questions and it is difficult to imagine starting a design project without the essential analysis completed.

Chuck Hodell,
ISD from the Ground Up: A No-Nonsense Approach to Instructional Design (2nd ed.)

Here's a summary of what's involved in each stage:

- *Analysis.* Every project, large or small, begins with questions. Those questions are intended to gather the information needed to clarify the reasons for undertaking the project, determine the likelihood of achieving the desired results, and figure out what it will take to move from idea to reality. Embarking on a project without that information is like entering a dark tunnel without a flashlight: you can't see where you're going, don't know what you'll encounter along the way, and aren't sure what you'll find when you reach the other end. The goal of analysis in a training project is to discover whether training is really needed and what the outcome should be; collect information that will help you design a program to achieve that outcome in the most cost-effective way; and determine who needs to be involved in the design process.

- *Design.* During this stage, you and your team zoom in on the details and prepare a detailed outline or design document that will guide you through the development process. The tasks include writing the learning objectives that specify what people will be able to do when training is completed; identifying the delivery method or methods that will be most likely to help learners achieve the objectives; identifying specific program content and planning the learning activities; and deciding how the program will be evaluated. In some situations, you might find that it would be more efficient and cost-effective to adapt an existing program or purchase a program off the shelf than to develop a new program from scratch.

- *Development.* The design document is a blueprint that guides the development process. During this stage, you will develop or manage the development of the materials needed to run the program, such as a facilitator script and participant handouts; e-learning modules; videos; assessments; job aids; self-study workbooks; game materials—whatever the program requires. Depending on the size, scope, and importance of the program, as well as the time you have available, you might run a "pilot" to identify changes that need to be made before the program is ready to go.

- *Implementation:* This stage is where the rubber meets the road. All the care that you've taken in previous stages pays off when the program rolls out. There's a lot to do in this stage—schedule training and notify participants; arrange for materials, equipment, and training rooms; prepare for training sessions; and, finally, deliver the program. The more attention you pay to the details, the more successful the training is likely to be.

- *Evaluation:* When a doctor prescribes medication to lower a patient's blood pressure, there is only one way to know whether the medication is working: by following up. The doctor's question, "How well is this working?" is the same one that you need to ask about your training programs. Ongoing evaluation is crucial to making sure that training is and remains necessary, relevant, effective, and a good return on investment. Although "Evaluation" appears at the end of the ADDIE acronym, the basis for evaluating the program is established when you write the learning objectives, and the results of the evaluation may lead to a return to earlier stages so the program can be improved.

3. Analyzing the Need

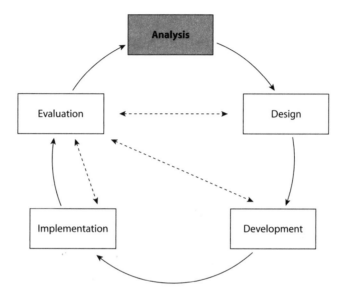

The Analysis Stage of the ADDIE Model

Throwing resources at problems or opportunities is like throwing a chocolate pie at the wall and hoping that some of it will stick: the action is more likely to create a mess than an improvement; furthermore, it is a waste of good resources.

Kavita Gupta, with Catherine M. Sleezer and Darlene F. Russ-Eft,
A Practical Guide to Needs Assessment (2nd ed.)

Check What You Know

Which statements are accurate about the analysis stage of ADDIE?

1. _____ It's important to be careful not to ask too many questions because you can easily be overwhelmed with information.
2. _____ The information gathered during the analysis stage provides the basis for evaluating the program's success.
3. _____ When the need for training is clear, you can skip the analysis stage or do it very quickly.
4. _____ One question to answer during this stage is whether it is really important to change the existing situation.
5. _____ One objective in this stage is to go beyond the assumptions that have already been made.

Analyzing anything—the screeching sound a car makes when the steering wheel is turned to the left, a child's difficulty in reading, the reasons why an election was won or lost, or the apparent need for a training program— requires asking lots and lots of questions. The objective is to go beyond the obvious into the unknown—beyond the assumptions that have already been made, beyond what's readily apparent—to determine what's really going on and what really needs to be done. When it comes to instructional design, many trainers make the mistake of stopping at the first round of questions, which might appear to support the initial assumption that training is needed, instead of probing more and more deeply until they have enough information to make informed decisions. While I've often regretted asking too few questions during this process, I cannot remember a time when I've asked too many.

The people from whom you gather information during this stage include those who requested the training, others who are knowledgeable about the situation and the subject, and anyone else who has some kind of stake in the desired outcome. Those people might include the organization's managers and executives, the people to whom the participants report (assuming that the participants have already been identified), people and teams in other areas of the organization, internal and external customers, and the participants themselves. Methods for collecting information include in-person and telephone interviews, focus groups, surveys and questionnaires, assessments, and observations.

There are several basic questions that the analysis seeks to answer: Is there really a need for training? Can the desired outcome be achieved in a different, and perhaps less expensive, way? Is achieving the desired outcome worth the cost? If it turns out that training is needed, the analysis provides information that is essential for designing a program that meets learners' needs while addressing the stakeholders' interests and concerns; establishing where the training falls in the organization's priorities; determining what resources are available; and identifying who needs to be involved in designing the program. The information gathered during this stage also provides a baseline that will be used to measure the success of the program after it has been delivered.

It's impossible to identify everything you need to know at the start of a training project or to specify the order in which questions should be asked. But here's an overview of the kinds of questions you generally need to ask:

- Why does training appear to be needed? What needs to change? What is the desired outcome?

- What's the reason for the current situation? What are the root cause(s) of the gap between the situation as it is now and the desired outcome?

- How important is it to change the existing situation? How will changing the situation help the organization achieve its strategic goals? What is likely to happen if nothing is done?

- What is the root cause of the gap between the current situation and the desired outcome? Is training the best way to close that gap? What other ways might there be to achieve the same goal?

- How quickly does the situation need to change? How urgent is this training?

- Who are the stakeholders? Who has an interest in achieving the desired outcome? Whose approval and support are needed?

- What are the constraints on the ways in which the desired outcome can be achieved?

- Who are the people who will participate in this training? What are the learners' characteristics?

- Who needs to be involved in the process of designing this training program? What roles will each of those people play?

*There is a mental (first) creation, and a physical (second) creation.
The physical creation follows the mental, just as a building
follows a blueprint . . . . Begin with the End in Mind means to
begin each day, task, or **project** [emphasis added] with a clear
vision of your desired direction and destination.*

Steven Covey,
www.stevencovey.com

What Change Is Needed? What's the Desired Outcome?

As you learned in Chapter 1, the purpose of training is to effect change—to close a performance gap between things as they are and things as they should be. Training programs are often triggered by a vague idea that something needs to change: "We need to do something about all the time that people are wasting in meetings." But that idea is just a starting point. You need to know much more about the current situation and the desired outcome so you can identify the gap between them and determine the best way to close it.

Start by trying to find out as much as possible about what's going on. Some questions might be: "Why and when do team leaders hold meetings? Who calls those meetings? Who runs them? What goes on during meetings? After meetings?" Try to find out what's not working (meetings start late, have no clear purpose or agenda, discussions go off track, team members have trouble reaching decisions, and so forth). Solidify the vague idea that change is needed into a vivid, concrete description of the destination: "We want team leaders to hold meetings only when they are necessary and use meeting time productively."

What Are the Root Cause(s) of the Current Situation?

Sometimes the reasons for the gap between the current situation and the desired outcome become clear fairly quickly: safety procedures have been revised and shop foremen need to know what operational changes to make; sales associates who work outside of the corporate office are using an old tracking system and their software needs to be replaced. But things are not always as clear as they first appear, and what seems to be the reason for the gap might actually be only a symptom. For example, it might appear that team leaders are holding unnecessary meetings because they don't know how to decide when meetings should be held. But further investigation reveals an important but overlooked fact: the team leaders are under the impression that they are expected to hold regular weekly, biweekly, or monthly meetings, and so they do, even when there is nothing important to discuss. Thus, an easy, quick way to reduce the number of unnecessary meetings would be to correct that misperception.

THINK ABOUT IT

In which of these situations might it *not* be worth the time and money to change the current situation?

1. _____ A small nonprofit health care organization is replacing its manual client tracking system with sophisticated software and wants everyone in the organization to switch to the new system within three months.
2. _____ The manager of the product development division of a large corporation that is planning a reorganization has requested training in team building to help the teams in her division work together more effectively.
3. _____ The CEO of a consulting firm has told the head of human resources that he wants to see significant improvement in the proposal writing skills of the three mid-level managers who are primarily responsible for soliciting new business.

How Important Is It to Change the Existing Situation?

Organizations sometimes devote scarce resources to training that isn't actually needed because they fail to ask, "What is likely to happen if we do nothing—if we just leave things as they are?"

I once had an experience that highlighted the importance of that question. I was conducting a workshop for employees in a financial services firm. The workshop was designed to help them write summaries of governmental regulations that impacted the way that the firm conducted its business.

Five minutes into the workshop I was stunned to learn that the company was in the midst of a merger—a fact that had been known to the manager who had hired me. Several of the participants told me that they expected layoff notices momentarily; those who hoped to stay on said that their responsibilities would probably change.

The company had already paid for the training facility and for my services, so we made the best of the situation: we spent the day on general business writing skills that participants could use no matter where they ended up. But I wondered about the extremely short-sighted manager who decided that his staff needed training but obviously never stopped to ask whether the investment in that training would be worthwhile for the organization. Although training that prepares people for change and helps them manage that change can be very useful, trainers should remain alert for indications, such as impending reorganizations, change initiatives, mergers, and economic downturns, that the idea for training should be reconsidered.

Is Training the Best Way to Achieve the Desired Outcome?

Instruction is only one of several possible solutions to problems of human performance. . . . It is quite possible to construct a magnificent course that nobody needs. . . .

Robert F. Mager,
Preparing Instructional Objectives

Training programs can be costly and time-consuming to develop and deliver. As you move through the analysis stage, be alert for indications that there might be other ways to achieve the desired outcome: Would a change in procedures, better equipment or software, more information, or a few job aids accomplish the same goal? How difficult is it to learn what needs to be learned? Is an expensive formal training program necessary? Could the same outcome be achieved with some on-the-job coaching? Keep in mind that it's hard to stop an engine once it's gotten up steam. Make sure that training is the best way to get the job done *before* beginning the time-consuming process of designing and developing a training program.

THINK ABOUT IT

Which of the training needs described below seems to be urgent? Which of these needs could probably wait until other priorities are taken care of?

1. An electronics firm is planning to launch a complex new product in six weeks. The members of the firm's sales team need to learn the features and functions of the prototype so they can explain the benefits of the product and demonstrate its use to prospective purchasers.

    _____ Urgent   _____ Not urgent

2. As part of its initiative to provide development opportunities to employees, an insurance company has decided to provide leadership training that will prepare high-performers to move into managerial positions as those positions open up.

    _____ Urgent   _____ Not urgent

3. A restaurant chain with three locations in the same city has been the target of several robberies during the past month. The employees need training in security procedures.

    _____ Urgent   _____ Not urgent

How Urgent Is This Training?

If the hard drive of your personal laptop computer crashes, you need to get it fixed right away (and hope you can recover your important data). But if the computer is only getting sluggish, you might be able to continue working until you have the time and money to take it in for repair.

In the same way, some training is urgent, and some can wait until other priorities have been taken care of and there is sufficient time and money to address them. Sometimes a training need is urgent because it is time-dependent: people need to get up to speed on a new system, new regulations or procedures are about to take effect, or a new product is about to be launched. Sometimes it is urgent because the consequences of not addressing a problem right away could be serious. For a company that is experiencing a high number of accidents, safety training would rise to the top of the priority list. A dysfunctional team that consistently fails to meet deadlines, holding up other teams' work, needs some kind of intervention, possibly training, before everyone gets too far behind.

The urgency of training not only establishes its priority, but it can also limit the choice of delivery methods. A sophisticated e-learning or print self-paced program would take much longer to develop than a short workshop with a few handouts or on-the-job training supported by job aids.

Who Are the Stakeholders?

An important part of the analysis stage of ADDIE is identifying the stakeholders, including the people whose approval and support are needed during the design and development process. Every instructional designer has seen perfectly good and badly needed training programs delayed or sidetracked because a key stakeholder didn't see it until it was ready to roll out and then insisted on changes that required going back to the drawing board. (After that happened to me a few times, I changed my client contract to include approval checkpoints that specified several stages at which I would require decision-makers' review and approval before moving forward.)

Stakeholders are people who have an interest in the training project and its outcome and whose support is essential for the program to succeed. Key stakeholders are the people who requested the training and the decision-makers who provide the resources. They include the participants' managers, whose support for the program can be critical—managers who do not see themselves as having a stake in the training effort might find other things for their employees to do on training day or undermine the training effort in other ways. Stakeholders might also include a board of directors, internal and external customers, and others.

It's important to identify the stakeholders early in the process. Getting the right people involved as early as possible helps you avoid problems such as those described above. Make sure that all the stakeholders understand the purpose of the program, how the training will benefit them and the organization, and that you need their ideas and support for the program to be a success.

What Are the Constraints?

Everything would be easier if we could always do things exactly the way we wanted to do them—at least, that's what we sometimes think. But in the real world we are always limited in some way: we don't have enough money, we don't have enough time, other people have different priorities and points of view than our own. To achieve any goal, we need to work with the situation that exists, not the situation as we would like it to be.

Think about all the factors that are likely to affect the way in which the desired outcome is achieved. What's the budget? How much time do you have available? What facilities, equipment, and expertise will you have access to? What are the ways in which organizational culture and politics might impact the training design?

What Are the Learners' Needs and Characteristics?

The more you know about the people who will participate in the training program, the better able you will be to meet their specific needs. An important part of the analysis stage is to find out as much about the group of people for whom this training is intended as you can. The questions include the following:

- *How many people will be trained?* The size of the target audience affects many of the decisions you'll make about the type of program to develop.

- *Do the learners already know about this training?* Will they be a self-selecting group, or is this training required? If it's required, how are people likely to feel about the training—Will they understand its importance? See the value to themselves?

- *Are the learners a diverse or cohesive group?* Do they have approximately the same amount of prior knowledge and skill level? Similar objectives for training?

- *What previous experiences have participants had with training?* Have they participated in previous programs? Is this a group that welcomes training or avoids it?

- *Have participants expressed a preference for one kind of training over another?* For example, participants might say that they prefer e-learning over workshops, or vice-versa. Although their preferences should not dictate the type of program you develop, it's important to take them into consideration when you are weighing alternatives.

- *Where are participants located? What kinds of time do they have available for training?* Are they all in one place, or scattered around the globe? Can they free up large blocks of time for training, or can they make only an hour or two at a time available?

When Training Is Mandated

Mandated training programs are those that people have no choice about attending. Training might be required for safety reasons, by government regulation, by licensing boards, or by company policy. It's helpful to know when training is mandatory instead of voluntary because people who attend mandatory programs are sometimes resistant to training. They might have had experience with mandated programs that were little more than lectures followed by a test, and the content of those programs might not have appeared to be (or actually were not) relevant to their jobs. In those situations, it can take a special effort on the part of the trainer to get people's full attention and encourage them to participate actively.

Here are some ways in which you can make mandated training more successful:

- Make sure that the program is as learner-centered as possible. Plan activities that will engage and involve participants right from the beginning.
- Ensure that participants understand why the training is being held and how it will benefit them.
- Provide activities that help participants link what they are learning to what they already know.
- Give participants plenty of opportunities to voice their concerns about the program.

Who Needs to Be Involved in the Design Process?

Like the process of putting on a play, instructional design is a team activity. There are both practical and political considerations for involving a wide range of people, including management, participants, subject-matter experts, trainers, program developers, and others throughout the process. For one thing, there's a real value in the interplay between different ideas and points of view. For another, you will undoubtedly need expertise that you don't have yourself. And, as mentioned above, involving people in the process means that you are more likely to have support for the program when you need it.

Establish contact with everyone who needs to be involved. Make sure that everyone has a good understanding of the reasons and goals for the program, the constraints, the deadlines, and their roles in the process. Be sure to let people know why their participation is important and to respect their other priorities.

Francesca's Analysis Process

To determine whether the customer service reps need training, Francesca reviewed the results of a customer satisfaction survey that the organization had recently conducted. She then met with the customer service representatives' manager and several of their supervisors. Here are the kinds of questions that she asked:

- Are there problems with the way in which the customer service reps are handling telephone orders? What are those problems?
- What is the performance gap? What do the service reps need to know and be able to do differently? What do they already know? What skills do they already have?
- What are the root causes of the performance gap? Do service reps know how to handle the orders? Do they have the information they need?

(Continued)

Training Fundamentals: Pfeiffer Essential Guides to Training Basics.
Copyright © 2010 by John Wiley & Sons, Inc.
Reproduced by permission of Pfeiffer, an Imprint of Wiley. www.Pfeiffer.com

- Have new products been introduced recently? Is there anything in the working environment that might be making it difficult for them to handle orders properly?
- How important is it to close the performance gap? How would the company be impacted if nothing was done?
- How urgent is it to close the gap? Are the problems affecting relationships with customers? Creating unnecessary expense? Is there a built-in deadline, such as the launch of a new product or the date on which new regulations take effect?
- Would a workshop be the most cost-effective way to close the gap? Would something other than training, or another form of training, achieve the desired outcome?
- How many customer service reps need to be trained? How much time do they have available for training? Are they all in the same location or can they be brought to the same location for training?
- What experiences have the customer service reps had with training? Have they participated in similar training programs? Have they expressed a preference for any type of training?
- What resources are available for this training program? Is there a predetermined budget? What kinds of equipment, facilities, and expertise are available?
- What are the constraints on this training program? Have any decisions been made that determine the ways in which training can or cannot be delivered? Is there a limit on the number of hours participants will have available for training? Are resources limited? What is the budget?
- Who needs to be involved in the program design? Should the service reps and/or their manager be involved? A subject-matter expert? Customers? People from other areas of the organization, or from outside the organization?

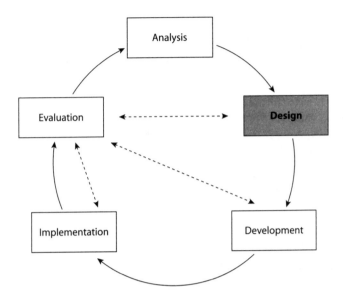

The Design Phase of the ADDIE Model

4. Writing the Learning Objectives

If you don't know where you are going you will end up some place you might not want to be. Instructional design is the art and science of building a roadmap that takes learners where they need to go.

Toni Hodges DeTuncq, "If You Don't Know Where You're Going, You Will Probably End Up Somewhere Else," in T.L. Gargiulo, A.M. Pangarkar, and T. Kirkwood (Eds.), *The Trainer's Portable Mentor*

Check What You Know

Which statements are accurate?

1. ___ A learning objective describes the process of instruction.
2. ___ A learning objective describes the intended result of instruction.
3. ___ A learning objective describes what people will be able to do when training is completed.
4. ___ A learning objective describes what people will know when training is completed.

Just as the instructional design is often compared to the process of planning a journey, learning objectives are often compared to a map. They show you where you are going and provide the signposts that keep you going in the right direction. I also like to think of learning objectives as forming the backbone, or spine, of a training program because they provide the solid structure that holds the program up. No matter what language you use to talk about learning objectives, however, what's important is to understand what they are and their function in the instructional design process.

- *What they are:* Written statements that express what learners will *be able to do* as a result of training and may also describe the conditions under which the objective will be achieved and the standard by which success will be measured.

- *What they do:* Provide the basis for determining what content and activities to include in the program, keep you focused on what the program is supposed to accomplish, tell the learners what they are trying to learn, and provide the criteria for measuring the program's success.

An objective is a description of a performance you want learners to be able to exhibit before you consider them competent. An objective describes an intended result of instruction, rather that the process of instruction itself.

Robert Mager,
Preparing Instructional Objectives

THINK ABOUT IT

A tennis player wants to improve her serve. Is the learning objective:

1. to learn to improve her serve?
2. to understand what changes to make in her serve?
3. to increase the number of times she gets the first serve in?

A useful learning objective includes language that clearly describes *behavior* or the *results of behavior*—something that can be observed and/or measured. You can't directly observe or measure what someone *learns* or *understands*. But you can observe or measure the *result* of that learning or understanding. Thus, the most useful learning objective for the tennis player would be "to increase the number of times she gets the first serve in."

Useful learning objectives include verbs that describe something that can be observed. You might have a pretty good idea of what someone is thinking by the look on his face, but you can't know for sure unless he tells you. That grimace might mean that he disagrees with you or that he has a toothache. You might think that someone understands what you have been saying, but she might have been nodding and smiling to be polite—you'll only know that she's understood when she says or does something that demonstrates understanding.

Training Fundamentals: Pfeiffer Essential Guides to Training Basics.
Copyright © 2010 by John Wiley & Sons, Inc.
Reproduced by permission of Pfeiffer, an Imprint of Wiley. www.Pfeiffer.com

THINK ABOUT IT

Circle the verbs in these columns that describe something that can be observed.

Think	State	Describe	Understand
Know	Identify	Demonstrate	Change (a Tire)
Explain	Appreciate	Change (Attitude)	Calculate
Circle (an Item)	Discuss (a Topic)	Write (a Report)	Feel (Satisfied)
Plan	Prepare	Agree	

Did you circle "State," "Describe," "Identify," "Explain," "Circle," "Discuss," Write," "Demonstrate," "Plan," "Prepare," "Change (a Tire)" and "Calculate"? You can watch people do those actions or observe the results of the actions they take. But you do not know what people think, feel, understand, or appreciate, or whether they have changed an attitude, unless they tell you or show you in some way.

The more specific that learning objectives are, the more useful they will be. Thus, some learning objectives need to include the conditions under which people will be expected to demonstrate that they have achieved the objective. Expecting a pianist to play a piece with the sheet music is different from expecting her to play it from memory alone. "With the sheet music" is a condition under which the pianist will be expected to demonstrate that she can play the piece. Including the conditions helps to focus the objective and can help avoid confusion about whether learners have actually achieved it.

Objectives with conditions might include the following:

- *"Use the online customer service manual* to respond accurately to customers' questions about our products."

- *"Given a case describing a current problem,* follow the problem-solving steps to come up with a solution."

- *"On a list of interview questions,* identify those that may be legally asked of job applicants."

Some objectives also need to include the standard for successful performance—a statement that answers the question, "How will we know whether learners have achieved the objectives? In other words, how will we measure success? As Robert Mager states in *Preparing Instructional Objectives,* "If you can specify the acceptable performance for each objective, you will have a standard against which to test your instruction . . . [and] determining whether your instruction is successful in achieving your instructional intent."

The standard should describe how well learners need to perform, how many widgets they need to produce, or how quickly they need to do what they are doing, as in these examples:

- For the customer service representative, "Using the online customer service manual, respond to customers' questions about our products *within five minutes with 95 percent accuracy."*

- For the tennis player, "Get the first serve in *30 percent of the time"* or "increase the number of times you get the first serve in *by 20 percent."*

The learning objectives for a training program do not come out of thin air. They are derived directly from the desired outcome of training: learning objectives are written statements that express what learners need to know and be able to do to achieve that outcome. Specifically, objectives state what knowledge learners need to acquire, what skills they need to learn or improve, or what attitudes they need to change. To return to the tennis player: The desired outcome of her learning program is to for her to be able to win more tennis games. One of her learning objectives is to get her serve in more often; another might be to reduce the number of errors she makes. If the desired outcome of a training program is to help team leaders run more productive team meetings, a learning objective might be for them to be able to prepare and distribute an agenda that meets the criteria on a checklist.

THINK ABOUT IT

Improve these learning objectives by rewriting them into statements that describe observable actions. If necessary, include a condition and describe how achievement will be measured.

1. Understand the importance of submitting monthly reports that follow the organization's guidelines.

    _____

    _____

    _____

    _____

2. Learn how to use PowerPoint to prepare slides for a presentation.

    _____

    _____

    _____

    _____

3. Respect differences in points of view when working with others to make decisions.

    _____

    _____

    _____

    _____

Enabling Objectives

In addition to learning objectives, the training program design process includes identifying what are often called "enabling" objectives—statements that describe what learners need to be able to do and/or know to achieve a learning objective. Enabling objectives, which are used to identify content, not to measure success, can be written more "loosely" than learning objectives, meaning that they do not necessarily have to describe actions that can be observed and they do not need to include standards or measurements of success. Perfectly appropriate enabling objectives might be, "Understand the kinds of questions that customers commonly ask" or "Recognize the relationship between the ball toss and a successful serve."

Quick Quiz

List the three to five key learning points from this chapter that will be most helpful to you.

_____

_____

_____

_____

_____

What's Next?

One of the decisions that must be made during the instructional design process is how to deliver the training. Making that decision requires considering such factors as the desired outcome, the learning objectives and type of learning, the characteristics of the target audience, the preferences of stakeholders, the budget, the available time and expertise, and more. In the next chapter, you'll learn about the different ways in which training is delivered and how to select the best option for a specific situation.

Apply What You Learn

Complete the worksheet at the end of this chapter to begin the process of designing your training program.

Answers to Exercises

Check What You Know

1. Where does the idea that training is needed come from?
    Training programs begin with an idea that something needs to change. The idea can come from almost anyone who perceives a need for change.
2. What are some of the reasons that people in organizations request training?
    Common reasons: new change initiatives, systems, regulations, procedures, policies, products, or services are introduced; there is a reorganization of some kind; individuals or teams fail to meet performance targets; morale is low; customer complaints or accidents are on the rise; deadlines are frequently missed; or other problems impact the organization's ability to achieve its goals.
3. Does a request for training mean that training is necessarily needed? Why or why not?
    Not necessarily. The person requesting training might have assumed that training was needed. In fact, change might actually not be needed or there might be another, better, way to achieve necessary change.

Check What You Know

Which statements are accurate about the analysis stage of ADDIE?

1. ___ It's important to be careful not to ask too many questions because you can easily be overwhelmed with information.
2. _X_ The information gathered during the analysis stage provides the basis for evaluating the program's success.
3. ___ When the need for training is clear, you can skip the analysis stage or do it very quickly.
4. _X_ One question to answer during this stage is whether it is really important to change the existing situation.
5. _X_ One objective in this stage is to go beyond the assumptions that have already been made.

• •

THINK ABOUT IT

In which of these situations might it *not* be worth the time and money to change the current situation?

1. ___ A small nonprofit health care organization is replacing its manual client tracking system with sophisticated software and wants everyone in the organization to switch to the new system within three months.
2. _X_ The manager of the product development division of a large corporation that is planning a reorganization has requested training in team building to help the teams in her division work together more effectively. *It is probably not worth the time and money to provide team-building training for a team that might no longer be together in a few months.*

(Continued)

3. ___ The CEO of a consulting firm has told the head of human resources that he wants to see significant improvement in the proposal writing skills of the three mid-level managers who are primarily responsible for soliciting new business.

THINK ABOUT IT

Which of the training needs described below seems to be urgent? Which of the needs could probably wait until other priorities are taken care of?

1. An electronics firm is planning to launch a complex new product in six weeks. The members of the firm's sales team need to learn the features and functions of the prototype so they can explain the benefits of the product and demonstrate its use to prospective purchasers.

   __X__ Urgent_____ Not urgent

2. As part of its initiative to provide development opportunities to employees, an insurance company has decided to provide leadership training that will prepare high-performers to move into managerial positions as those positions open up.

   ___ Urgent __X__ Not urgent

3. A restaurant chain with three locations in the same city has been the target of several robberies during the past month. The employees need training in security procedures.

   __X__ Urgent___ Not urgent

Check What You Know

Which statements are accurate?

1. ___ A learning objective describes the process of instruction.
2. _X_ A learning objective describes the intended result of instruction.
3. _X_ A learning objective describes what people will be able to do when training is completed.
4. ___ A learning objective describes what people will know when training is completed.

THINK ABOUT IT

A tennis player wants to improve her serve so that she can get more first serves in. Is the learning objective:

1. ___ to learn to improve her serve?
2. ___ to understand what changes to make in her serve?
3. _X_ to increase the number of times she gets the first serve in?

THINK ABOUT IT

Improve these learning objectives by rewriting them into statements that describe observable actions. If necessary, include a condition and describe how achievement will be measured.

Here are some suggested objectives. Yours are likely to differ, but they should describe an observable action and, if necessary, include a condition and describe how achievement will be measured.

1. Understand the importance of submitting monthly reports that follow the organization's guidelines.

   Given a copy of the organization's guidelines for monthly reporting, submit monthly reports that follow those guidelines.

2. Learn how to use PowerPoint to prepare slides for a presentation.

   Given a job aid, content information, and a PowerPoint design template, prepare PowerPoint slides to support a sixty-minute presentation. All slides will meet the criteria on the job aid.

3. Respect differences in points of view when working with others to make decisions.

   During team decision-making meetings, listen while others give their opinions and ask questions as needed to clarify.

Worksheet: Training Program Design Planning

Brief description of project: _____

_____

_____

1. Is Training Needed?

Current situation:

_____

_____

Desired outcome:

_____

_____

Root cause(s) of gap between current situation and desired outcome:

_____

_____

What is likely to happen if the gap is not closed?

_____

_____

_____

(Continued)

Is training the best way, or one of the ways, to achieve the desired outcome? What alternatives are there?

_____

_____

2. Key Stakeholders

Name or describe each key stakeholder or group of stakeholders. What interests does each stakeholder have in this training?

Stakeholder 1

_____

_____

Stakeholder 2

_____

_____

Stakeholder 3

_____

_____

Stakeholder 4

_____

_____

_____

3. Constraints

What are the constraints on this training project? (limits on money, time, facilities, equipment, expertise, and other resources; stakeholder preferences and political considerations)

_____

_____

_____

_____

_____

4. Learners

What are the characteristics of the learners? (location, size of group, how selected, preferences, available time, etc.)

_____

_____

_____

_____

_____

5. Design Team

Who needs to be involved in the design process? (managers, participants, subject-matter experts, training professionals, programmers, etc.)

_____

_____

_____

_____

_____

(Continued)

6. Learning Objectives

Write three to five learning objectives that express what people will be able to do when training is completed. Include conditions and standards if necessary:

Objective 1:

_____

_____

_____

Objective 2:

_____

_____

_____

Objective 3:

_____

_____

_____

Objective 4:

_____

_____

_____

Objective 5:

_____

_____

_____

4

Deciding on Delivery Options

Check What You Know

Carleton is part of a training team that is designing a training program to help new team leaders manage projects so they stay on track, meet deadlines, and achieve specific goals. What are all the ways you can think of in which this training might be delivered?

_____

_____

_____

_____

Training professionals share one characteristic that sometimes gets in the way of common sense: We love to learn about and experiment with new things. That's one of the most helpful characteristics we can have, of course, but sometimes it causes us to lose sight of the goal, which should be coming up with the best way for people to learn. Instead, we sometimes latch onto complicated new ideas and expensive new technology and plow ahead, when what we really need to do is examine all the options available so that we can come up with the most efficient, most effective way to deliver training that achieves our organization's goals and meets our learners' needs.

Here's what you'll find in this chapter:

- An overview of the ways in which training programs are delivered
- The differences among types of learning programs
- Methods by which training is commonly delivered
- How to decide on the best delivery option or options for a given situation

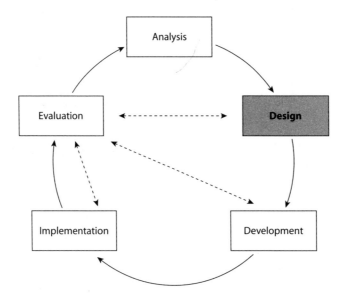

1. Overview of Delivery Methods

Check What You Know

How much do you already know about the different options for delivering training? Which statements are accurate?

1. _____ Even in this highly technological age, a live, in-person workshop is still the most common way to deliver training.
2. _____ On-the-job training should only be used when there is no budget for a formal training program.
3. _____ Virtual (web-based) workshops offer a cost-effective way to provide training when participants are widely disbursed.
4. _____ e-Learning programs are an excellent way to train large numbers of people on almost any subject.
5. _____ Study groups can be used to extend the value of self-directed learning programs.

There have been enormous changes in the workplace during the past few decades. Increasing numbers of people now work from remote locations or telecommute from home. Nearly everyone uses technology, and that technology changes in a blink of an eye. People start new jobs or take on new responsibilities more often than ever before, and they are under increasing pressure to get more done in less time—which means that they have less time available for training. All those changes are having profound effects on the ways in which training is delivered, and we will see even greater changes in the next decade. So it might come as a surprise to learn that, according to ASTD's *2007 State of the Industry Report*, more than 65 percent of training is still delivered through live instructor-led workshops and seminars, commonly referred to as "classroom" training. In fact, workshops are the first thing that many people think of when they think of training.

There are many reasons why classroom training is still the most common delivery method. The workshop format is familiar—we've all spent many years learning in classrooms. Workshops can be delivered without the need for costly technology that itself may require training to learn. And workshops offer something that even the most sophisticated e-learning programs are not

Training Fundamentals: Pfeiffer Essential Guides to Training Basics.
Copyright © 2010 by John Wiley & Sons, Inc.
Reproduced by permission of Pfeiffer, an Imprint of Wiley. www.Pfeiffer.com

able to provide: the immediate, face-to-face human interaction that can be crucial to learning.

But even though workshops remain, for the moment, the most common training delivery method, there are lots of others. As a well-rounded training professional, you need to have all those methods in your bag of tricks so you can make good decisions about how best to help specific learners achieve specific objectives in a specific situation.

2. Three Types of Learning Programs

One of the first things to know about the ways in which training is delivered is that there are really only three types of learning programs: synchronous training, in which people are learning at the same time; asynchronous training, in which they are not necessarily learning at the same time; and combinations of the two.

Quick Quiz

Match the statement to the type of learning program

(S) Synchronous   (A) Asynchronous   (C) Combination

1. _____ A workshop conducted in a classroom, where all the participants and the trainer are in the same location at the same time.
2. _____ A distance learning program in which participants receive assignments by e-mail and send in their completed assignments for feedback.
3. _____ A self-directed e-learning program in which participants meet once a week in a chat room to discuss what they are learning.
4. _____ A virtual classroom, for which participants log onto a website and use a telephone or audio link to interact with the trainer and the other participants.
5. _____ A podcast that learners can listen to while they are driving, taking a walk, or working out.
6. _____ On-the-job training during which an experienced employee demonstrates how to do a task and gives the learner feedback as he or she tries it.

Synchronous Training

Synchronous training most commonly refers to training that is delivered by a live instructor or facilitator to a group of people, all of whom are present in the same time at the same place. Thus, a live, in-person workshop would be synchronous training. But synchronous training also includes:

- On-the-job training, whereby individuals learn under the guidance of a supervisor or experienced colleague
- Study groups, which allow small groups of people to learn together in person, in a virtual meeting room, via telephone or an audio link, or in a chat room without an instructor or facilitator
- Workshops in which most of the learners are present at the same time but some are attending via a phone or video link
- Live virtual training conducted in a web-based training room for learners who are present at the same time but are not in the same place

The most important characteristic of synchronous training is that participants are able to communicate and interact with the instructor and one another in real time. This type of training is the best—sometimes the only—choice when learning requires that participants be able to share information and ideas, ask questions, and work together on learning activities. But it takes careful planning to schedule training at a time when all participants can attend and the necessary facilities and equipment are available. Live, in-person workshops can involve significant costs for participant and/or instructor travel, facility rental, and/or special equipment, and live web-based workshops require web collaboration software and the expertise to use it.

Asynchronous Training

In asynchronous training, there is no real-time interaction—sometimes, no interaction at all—between learners and between learners and trainer. Participants may complete instructor-delivered assignments or self-paced lessons in e-learning programs, on the web, or in printed materials at times and locations of their own choosing. They might or might not have trainers, coaches, supervisors, or others available for guidance and questions.

Training Fundamentals: Pfeiffer Essential Guides to Training Basics.
Copyright © 2010 by John Wiley & Sons, Inc.
Reproduced by permission of Pfeiffer, an Imprint of Wiley. www.Pfeiffer.com

Groups of learners who are taking the same program might communicate with one another by e-mail, threaded discussions, wikis, and/or bulletin or discussion boards. The program might or might not be supervised and monitored.

A clear advantage to asynchronous training is the flexibility in scheduling. There is no need for trainers to analyze schedules to find times when groups can meet, nor for learners to juggle their schedules so they can attend a workshop. Some forms of asynchronous training, such as printed workbooks or online assignments, are relatively inexpensive to produce or purchase. Programs can often be customized to meet individual needs. Asynchronous training, however, is not the best option in situations that benefit from extensive interaction and feedback.

Synchronous vs. Asynchronous Learning

Synchronous	Asynchronous
Offers real-time communication and collaboration between trainer and learners, and between learners	Lets learners work at a place, time, and pace of their choosing
Requires trainer and learners to be available at the same time and usually in the same place	Learner and trainer schedules do not need to be coordinated
Requires that learners take blocks of time away from their work	Learners can complete the training in small chunks at convenient times
Trainer may be able to make changes in content and structure at the last minute or on the spot	Fixed content, structure, and format—difficult to make changes
Depending on subject, location of learners, and other factors, can be developed quickly for relatively little cost	Some forms can be expensive and time-consuming to develop
Can be customized for specific learners	Delivers the same content in a consistent way to every learner

3. Common Delivery Methods

Check What You Know

Below are descriptions of methods by which training
is delivered and situations in which training is needed.
Considering cost, effectiveness, and practicality, which training delivery
method or methods would be best for each situation? Why?

A. Live workshop (learners and the trainer are together in the same place
    at the same time)
B. Self-directed e-learning (people use a computer to learn on their own,
    at a location, place, and time of their choosing)
C. Self-paced workbook (people use a print workbook to learn on their own)
D. Podcasts (brief audio or video programs that learners can listen to or
    watch on a computer or a mobile device)
E. On-the-job training (people learn a task or job by doing it with the
    guidance of an experienced person)
F. Live virtual workshop (learners and the trainer meet at the same time
    via the web and audio links)

1. _____ A rapidly growing biotech company needs to provide leadership
    training to approximately seventy mid-level managers in its home office.
2. _____ More than one hundred environmental engineers, who work
    for a company with offices in five Western U.S. states and are often out
    in the field, need training in report writing skills.
3. _____ A bank that hires two or three loan processors at a time needs
    to provide training that will quickly get the new hires up to speed on
    loan processing procedures.
4. _____ Grocery clerks at a chain with ten stores in different cities need
    to learn how to operate a new checkout system that is being installed
    in four weeks.
5. _____ The product support division of a large electronics corporation
    needs to provide periodic product updates to its employees, who are
    widely disbursed throughout the United States and Asia.

Training Fundamentals: Pfeiffer Essential Guides to Training Basics.
Copyright © 2010 by John Wiley & Sons, Inc.
Reproduced by permission of Pfeiffer, an Imprint of Wiley. www.Pfeiffer.com

A training delivery method is a tool for helping people learn. We all know the importance of choosing the right tool for a job—when you need to apply a coat of paint, you need a brush, not a screwdriver. In the same way, there's a better chance of achieving a specific training objective when you use the right delivery method. Being able to do that requires an understanding of the most common methods, including what situations they are best suited for.

Live, In-Person Workshops

As mentioned above, live, instructor-led training where participants and the instructor are in the same place at the same time is still the most common form of training. There are several advantages to this delivery method. Perhaps the most important is that it offers the greatest opportunity for interaction. Working together in a training room, participants can learn from one another as well as from the trainer; ask questions and discuss issues; share ideas; and participate in interactive activities that help them learn. Classroom training also offers a great deal of flexibility—changes to the content and activities can be made at the last minute, even on the spot, to tailor the training to the needs of a specific group. And while high-tech equipment and professionally prepared materials can enhance the learning experience, the only real requirements for most workshops are a trainer, a group, and a place in which they can meet.

Workshops can be held anywhere that a suitable room is available: in meeting rooms at the participants' workplace or in an off-site location such as a hotel, conference center, or local college. Participants might be part of

> ## What's in a Name
>
> Like any other field, training has its own terminology, and different terms are often used to refer to the same thing. A workshop essentially means training that is delivered by a trainer to a group of learners who are all together at the same time and in the same place. Workshops are often called "seminars," "classes," "courses," and "classroom training." Trainers are sometimes called "facilitators," "instructors," and "teachers." For consistency, we'll generally use the terms "workshops" and "trainers" in this book.
>
> For more on the terminology used in training, see Chapter 7.

the same team, from different areas of the organization, or from different organizations. The sessions might be conducted by an in-house trainer or by an outside facilitator. It is increasingly common for some participants to attend via the telephone or a video link.

THINK ABOUT IT

For which of these topics would a live, in-person workshop would be the best training delivery method?

1. _____ An introduction to PowerPoint for marketing associates
2. _____ Strategic planning for an executive team
3. _____ Giving useful performance feedback for new managers
4. _____ Updated expense report procedures for auditors
5. _____ How to prepare a quarterly budget for team leaders

Virtual Workshops

One of the most useful advances in training technology has been the development of virtual meeting rooms—websites on which a trainer and a group of participants simultaneously log on and join in a telephone conference call or use an audio link to talk with one another in real time. Virtual workshops offer many of the same opportunities as traditional workshops for participants to interact with the trainer and with one another. Learners can discuss issues, see demonstrations, ask questions, and participate in interactive learning activities—although those interactions are necessarily limited by the constraints of the technology.

The obvious advantage is that people can participate from anywhere in the world, reducing the cost and time needed for workshop participants to travel. But there are disadvantages to virtual workshops, as well. They are not as flexible as traditional workshops and it's harder to customize them on the spot to meet learners' specific needs. They need to be shorter than traditional workshops—material needs to be broken up so that it can be delivered in modules that are no longer than sixty to ninety minutes each. Conducting virtual training requires both the technology and the ability needed to use it. They are not as effective as live, in-person workshops for situations in which trainers and participants need to establish trust and rapport so they can address sensitive issues. It is harder in a virtual workshop for trainers to capture and hold participants' attention; without the visual cues provided in a physical training room, trainers may not know when people are confused—or when they are checking their e-mail.

One advantage of virtual workshops over live in-person training is that the workshop can easily be recorded for later viewing by people who could not attend or who would like to review what they learned.

THINK ABOUT IT

In which situation(s) would a traditional workshop be best? In which would a virtual workshop be an appropriate alternative?

(T) Traditional workshop   (V) Virtual workshop

1. _____ A dysfunctional team needs to learn what it can do to function more productively.
2. _____ New managers need to learn the basic principles of delegating a job.
3. _____ Retail store managers need to learn new security procedures.

Self-Paced Print

A self-paced print learning program is one in which learners work at their own pace, at times of their own choosing, to read content and complete exercises in a workbook. When I was in college, I used a self-paced workbook in lieu of a class for a course in statistics, and at my first training job, I learned the basics of instructional design by completing a self-paced workbook that had been developed by my manager. You might also have used self-paced print programs to learn a variety of topics.

Even in today's highly technological world, a self-paced workbook can still offer an inexpensive and efficient way to deliver training to large numbers of people when the topic doesn't require much, if any, interaction with others. Programs can be designed to provide learners with feedback as they work, and self-paced workbooks can be easily combined with other delivery methods, such as workshops and online training. They can be printed, like books, or delivered electronically as PDF files that learners can print out and carry with them to work on whenever and wherever it's convenient.

One disadvantage of self-paced print is that today's workers might consider a self-paced workbook an old-fashioned way to go about learning something. Another is that there is little flexibility to adapt printed workbooks to learners' specific needs. Like other forms of self-directed learning, self-paced print programs also require a certain amount of motivation and follow-through on the learners' part, so they work best when they are monitored or supervised in some way.

● ●

THINK ABOUT IT

Can you think of a topic and a situation for which self-paced print might be the right training delivery method?

_____

_____

● ●

Self-Directed e-Learning

You already know that e-learning refers to self-paced learning that is delivered electronically. An online tutorial for learning to use a software program such as Excel or PowerPoint is a self-directed e-learning program. So is a game or simulation in which learners practice doing a task or identifying and solving a problem.

Not surprisingly, learning delivered via computer is the fastest-growing method of delivering training. More and more of us now turn to our computers and electronic devices whenever we want information. Well-designed e-learning programs provide lots of the interactivity and feedback that are essential to learning, and they can be designed to tailor instruction to meet individual needs. Learners can use e-mail and web-based tools such as discussion boards, wikis, and blogs to collaborate with and support one another while they work. Self-directed e-learning can also be easily combined with other delivery methods.

Like self-paced print instruction, self-directed e-learning works best for subjects that don't require immediate human interaction. One disadvantage is that, while simple tutorials can be created using readily available software, sophisticated programs that provide learners with extensive practice and feedback can be very costly and time-consuming to develop.

THINK ABOUT IT

What are some topics that would lend themselves to e-learning?

_____

_____

Study Groups

Formal or informal study groups offer a relatively easy, low-cost way for people to learn together in person, in a virtual meeting room, or in a chat room. Although a trainer might be around to help them get started and to provide support, the participants work pretty much on their own. Study groups are an excellent, inexpensive way to extend the value of self-paced print and self-directed e-learning programs. Participants can discuss what they are learning, find answers to questions, add variety by doing some exercises as a group, and explore ways to apply what they learn on the job. Most study groups are small—three to ten people—and they work best when the group sets up a system for planning and scheduling meetings.

• •

THINK ABOUT IT

Describe a situation in which a study group could be used to provide training or support a training program:

_____

_____

• •

On-the-Job Training

If your first job was as a receptionist for a small company, a clerk at a local store, or a gas station attendant, chances are that you did not go through a formal training program. Instead, the manager or supervisor showed you around on your first day, perhaps assigning an experienced employee to explain the job and help you get started. You probably observed how the job was done, then tried it yourself under the supervision of the experienced person until you got it more or less right. You might have been given a set of instructions—a job aid—to help you remember what to do.

Training Fundamentals: Pfeiffer Essential Guides to Training Basics.
Copyright © 2010 by John Wiley & Sons, Inc.
Reproduced by permission of Pfeiffer, an Imprint of Wiley. www.Pfeiffer.com

On-the-job training, which is a perfect example of learning by doing, has been around ever since anyone learned to do a job. (Apprenticeships are on-the-job training.) It doesn't cost much and doesn't require much preparation. How effective it is, however, depends to a great degree on the nature of the job and the ability of the experienced person to be a good coach. The value of on-the-job training can be increased with clear learning objectives, checklists, and tests.

THINK ABOUT IT

Have you ever received on-the-job training? What did your "coach" do to help you learn? What would have made the training more effective?

_____

_____

_____

_____

Podcasts

People are constantly on the go these days, and they love to multitask. What better than learning while you're at the gym or waiting for a flight? Audio or video podcasts offer a quick, easy, inexpensive way to provide training that requires no interaction and no immediate feedback. Strictly speaking, podcasts deliver information, not training—there are no exercises, no discussions, no opportunity for practice or to ask questions. But these kinds of learning modules offer a cost-effective way to provide people with "just-in-time" information, such as updates on new products, guidelines, or tips. They can also help trainers make better use of valuable classroom time by providing some of the content before a workshop or between workshop sessions.

Videos

Like podcasts, videos that learners view on a computer, a hand-held electronic device, or a television monitor are primarily ways of delivering information. Unless videos are combined with other delivery methods, there is no opportunity for the learners to interact with the material. But videos can be a powerful, engaging way of presenting information. For example, videos can be used for demonstrations of ineffective or effective ways of doing things or in place of written case studies to stimulate workshop participants' thinking and get discussions started. For self-directed learning programs, videos can made more interactive by providing reflection questions and practice opportunities.

Technology has made it much easier and cheaper to develop simple videos. You don't need much technical expertise to use a webcam to record a demonstration, a panel discussion, an interaction, or a lecture. But even with today's technology, high-quality videos can still be expensive and time-consuming to produce. For many topics, however, there are many excellent off-the-shelf videos readily available, some of which include discussion guides that help you incorporate them into a training program.

THINK ABOUT IT

What are some ways in which podcasts and videos might be used to support a training program?

- Podcasts

_____

_____

- Videos

_____

_____

Blended Learning

As technology becomes more readily available, instructional designers are increasingly drawing on a variety of delivery methods to create the right programs to achieve specific goals. Blended learning refers to the process of combining different delivery methods into a cohesive program that meets the needs of different learners in different situations. A program that uses podcasts or videos to provide some of the content for a workshop is one form of blended learning. Others include using study groups to add interactivity to self-paced print or e-learning programs; on-the-job coaching that helps people transfer the learning from a workshop to their jobs; and the use of wikis and blogs to help learners share ideas, information, and best practices after a workshop.

The challenge when using blending learning is to make sure that all the components work together to provide a meaningful learning experience that helps people achieve the program's learning objectives. Accomplishing that goal requires careful design and attentive program management.

THINK ABOUT IT

For a training program on leadership skills for managers who work in different locations, describe some ways in which delivery methods might be combined into a blended learning program.

_____

_____

_____

_____

4. How to Decide on Delivery Options

Begin with the learner. Determine the desired outcome. Design training to help learners progress from where they are to where they ought to be. Adapt the delivery system to the characteristics of the learners and the content. Those are the essentials.

Harold D. Stolovitch and Erica J. Keeps,
Telling Ain't Training

Check What You Know

Carleton and his team have been reviewing options for delivering the project management training to team leaders.
What are some of the factors they need to consider? What are some of the questions they need to ask?

_____

_____

_____

_____

_____

_____

By the time you have completed the analysis stage of ADDIE and developed the learning objectives, you should have a pretty good idea about the best way to deliver the training. Budget or time considerations might have ruled out more expensive options, such as customized e-learning. The participants' dispersed locations might make a virtual workshop the most practical delivery method if the subject requires collaboration and interaction. The situation and subject matter might call for on-the-job training. A decision-maker whose support for the program is essential might have a preference for a live workshop. The numbers of people to be trained, their work responsibilities, and the nature of what they need to learn might dictate a self-paced print program.

Just as it's important not to assume that training is the best way to address a performance gap, it's important not to assume that the first delivery option that pops up is the best one. It's also important not to be led astray by tempting new technologies, because the most sophisticated and expensive method is not necessarily the one that is most likely to achieve the desired results.

Begin by considering the desired outcome and the learning objectives. Think about the participants' characteristics and preferences, the urgency of the program, and how many people need to be trained. If it appears that several delivery methods would work, choose the one or the combination that is the easiest, fastest, and requires the fewest resources. If you disagree with decision-makers' or learners' preferences, try to build a case for a method that you think is more likely to achieve results within the constraints of the situation.

To make the decision about how to deliver training, consider these kinds of factors:

- *The program goals and the learning objectives.* What is this program intended to accomplish? What changes are needed in the learners' behavior? An e-learning program might work very well if the goal is to help managers learn how to use new software for preparing budgets, but a program for helping them work with others to solve problems would be more effective in a live venue where they can interact.

- *What participants need to learn.* Do participants need to expand their knowledge? Learn new skills or improve skills they already have? Change their attitudes? Does what they need to learn require interactivity and discussion? Feedback? Demonstrations? Hands-on practice? A self-paced print program could work very well if the goal is to teach people to balance a checking account, but learning to change a tire on a truck probably requires live instruction.

- *The time frame.* When does training need to be completed? How long do you have to design, develop, and deliver the training? It's important to be realistic. If people need to be trained quickly, there might not be enough time to develop a good self-directed learning program, even if self-paced print or e-learning appears to be the best way to meet the learners' needs.

- *Available resources*. How much money do you have? What expertise is available? Can you obtain the equipment you'll need? The facilities? Delivery options are often limited by the budget. Just as it's important to be realistic about the time frame, you need to consider the resources carefully when deciding on delivery methods.

- *Where participants are located*. Are participants all in the same location? If not, would it be practical for them to travel? Even though a live, in-person workshop might be the ideal delivery method, you'll have to look at other options if participants are widely disbursed and cannot easily be brought together for training.

- *The number of people to be trained*. How many people need this training? How often will this program be repeated? Selecting the right delivery

Questions for Deciding What Delivery System to Use

- What are the goals? What is the program intended to accomplish?
- What do participants need to learn? Expand their knowledge? Learn or improve skills? Change their attitudes?
- How much interaction, practice, and feedback do they need?
- What's the time frame? When does training need to be completed?
- What resources are available? How much money? Expertise?
- Where are participants located? Are in the same location? Widely disbursed?
- How many people are to be trained? How often will the program be repeated?
- What preferences, if any, have managers, decision-makers, and/or participants expressed? Do you agree that those delivery methods are best?

Training Fundamentals: Pfeiffer Essential Guides to Training Basics.
Copyright © 2010 by John Wiley & Sons, Inc.
Reproduced by permission of Pfeiffer, an Imprint of Wiley. www.Pfeiffer.com

method(s) involves a business decision: determining whether the numbers of people to be trained justify the delivery cost. In most situations, it's only worth the expense of developing a sophisticated e-learning program if sufficient numbers of people will receive the training.

- *Preferences.* Have managers, decision-makers, and/or participants expressed a preference for a specific delivery method? People sometimes feel strongly about the ways in which training should be delivered. You might have to build the case for using a different method. When that's not possible, you may have to settle for a less than perfect fit, as long as you still believe that it will meet participants' needs and achieve the goals.

Quick Quiz

List the three to five key learning points from this chapter that will be most helpful to you.

_____

_____

_____

_____

_____

What's Next?

Once you have finished the Design stage of ADDIE, you've collected and sorted through a lot of information and made a lot of decisions. You know what the program is intended to achieve, what learners will be able to accomplish as a result of training, and how the program will be delivered. In the next chapter, you'll learn about the Development stage, during which you pull everything together by identifying and organizing the content, designing the learning activities, developing the materials, testing the program to make sure that everything works as planned, and determining how to evaluate the success of training.

Training Fundamentals: Pfeiffer Essential Guides to Training Basics.
Copyright © 2010 by John Wiley & Sons, Inc.
Reproduced by permission of Pfeiffer, an Imprint of Wiley. www.Pfeiffer.com

Apply What You Learn

Answer the questions below to think about the delivery
method or methods that would be best for your training project.

1. What are the goals? What is the program intended to accomplish?

_____

_____

_____

_____

2. What do participants need to learn?

☐ Expand their knowledge?

_____

_____

_____

_____

_____

☐ Learn or improve skills?

_____

_____

_____

_____

_____

(Continued)

☐ Change their attitudes?

_____

_____

_____

_____

_____

3. When does training need to be completed?

_____

4. What resources are available?

_____

_____

5. Where are participants located?

_____

6. How many people are to be trained?

_____

7. What preferences have managers, decision-makers, and/or participants expressed?

_____

_____

8. Which delivery system(s) would be best for the learners?

☐ live in-person workshop   ☐ podcast

☐ virtual workshop   ☐ other or blended learning
                                   (describe)
☐ self-directed e-learning
                                   _____
☐ self-paced print workbook
                                   _____
☐ on-the-job training

Answers to Exercises

Check What You Know

How much do you already know about the different options for delivering training? Which statements are accurate?

1. _X_ Even in this highly technological age, a live, in-person workshop is still the most common way to deliver training.
2. ___ On-the-job training should only be used when there is no budget for a formal training program.
3. _X_ Virtual (web-based) workshops offer a cost-effective way to provide training when participants are widely disbursed.
4. ___ e-Learning programs are an excellent way to train large numbers of people on almost any subject.
5. _X_ Study groups can be used to extend the value of self-directed learning programs.

Quick Quiz

Match the statement to the type of learning program

(S) Synchronous (A) Asynchronous (C) Combination

1. __S__ A workshop conducted in a classroom, where all the participants and the trainer are in the same location at the same time.
2. __A__ A distance learning program in which participants receive assignments by e-mail and send in their completed assignments for feedback.

(Continued)

Training Fundamentals: Pfeiffer Essential Guides to Training Basics.
Copyright © 2010 by John Wiley & Sons, Inc.
Reproduced by permission of Pfeiffer, an Imprint of Wiley. www.Pfeiffer.com

3. __C__ A self-directed e-learning program in which participants meet once a week in a chat room to discuss what they are learning.
4. __S__ A virtual classroom, for which participants log onto a website and use a telephone or audio link to interact with the trainer and the other participants.
5. __A__ A podcast that learners can listen to while they are driving, taking a walk, or working out.
6. __S__ On-the-job training during which an experienced employee demonstrates how to do a task and gives the learner feedback as he or she tries it.

Check What You Know

Below are descriptions of methods by which training is delivered and situations in which training is needed. Considering cost, effectiveness, and practicality, which training delivery method or methods would be best for each situation? Why?

A. Live workshop (learners and the trainer are together in the same place at the same time)
B. Self-directed e-learning (people use a computer to learn on their own, at a location, place, and time of their choosing)
C. Self-paced workbook (people use a print workbook to learn on their own)
D. Podcasts (brief audio or video programs that learners can listen to or watch on a computer or a mobile device)
E. On-the-job training (people learn a task or job by doing it with the guidance of an experienced person)
F. Live virtual workshop (learners and the trainer meet at the same time via the web and audio links)

Here are suggested training delivery methods for each situation, along with a brief rationale. Your answers might differ.

1. ___A___ A rapidly growing biotech company needs to provide leadership training to approximately seventy mid-level managers in its home office.

    Effective leadership training requires face-to-face interaction between the trainer and the participants, and between participants. Since the managers are all in one location, live, in-person workshops would probably be a practical way of providing training.

2. ___B, C, or F___ More than one hundred environmental engineers, who work for a company with offices in five Western U.S. states and are often out in the field, need training in report writing skills.

    Finding a time to bring these widely disbursed learners together is likely to be a logistical nightmare and involve a great deal of travel expense. Because learning report writing does not necessarily require collaboration, self-directed e-learning, or self-paced print instruction that includes opportunities for both practice and feedback might be a practical way to meet their needs. But virtual workshops, which allow people to attend from anywhere in the world, would have the advantage of allowing the engineers to ask questions of the trainer and work together on writing projects, thus helping them learn. Virtual workshops can also be recorded so that engineers who could not attend a workshop could watch one at a later time.

3. ___ B or E___ A bank that hires two or three loan processors at a time needs to provide training that will quickly get them up to speed on loan processing procedures.

    If the bank hires a significant number of loan processors over the course of a year, it might be worth the expense of developing an e-learning program. Otherwise, the most practical method would be on-the-job training.

    (Continued)

Training Fundamentals: Pfeiffer Essential Guides to Training Basics.
Copyright © 2010 by John Wiley & Sons, Inc.
Reproduced by permission of Pfeiffer, an Imprint of Wiley. www.Pfeiffer.com

4. ___A and/or E___ Grocery clerks at a chain with ten stores in different cities need to learn how to operate a new checkout system that is being installed in four weeks.

The most practical option might be for trainers to travel to each store as soon as the checkout system is installed to provide a short hands-on workshop so clerks can learn and practice the new system and ask questions about its use. Another option would be for a trainer to train store managers, who would then provide on-the-job training to their clerks.

5. ___D___ The product support division of a large electronics corporation needs to provide periodic product updates to its staff, who are widely disbursed throughout the United States and Asia.

Because product support staff are widely disbursed and they need only information, podcasts might be the easiest, least expensive way to provide the updates.

THINK ABOUT IT

For which of these topics would a live, in-person workshop would be the best training delivery method?

1. ___ An introduction to PowerPoint for marketing associates
2. _X_ Strategic planning for an executive team
3. _X_ Giving useful performance feedback for new managers
4. ___ Updated expense report procedures for auditors
5. ___ How to prepare a quarterly budget for team leaders

Training Fundamentals: Pfeiffer Essential Guides to Training Basics.
Copyright © 2010 by John Wiley & Sons, Inc.
Reproduced by permission of Pfeiffer, an Imprint of Wiley. www.Pfeiffer.com

THINK ABOUT IT

In which situation(s) would a traditional workshop be best? In which would a virtual workshop be an appropriate alternative?

(T) Traditional workshop   (V) Virtual workshop

1. ___T or V___ A dysfunctional team needs to learn what it can do to function more productively.
2. ___T or V___ New managers need to learn the basic principles of delegating a job.
3. ___T or V___ Retail store managers need to learn new security procedures.

5

Developing a Training Program and Planning the Program Evaluation

Check What You Know

For the customer representative training program, Francesca's team has identified the learning objectives and decided to deliver the training in a workshop. Now they are ready to develop the program and plan the program evaluation. What are some of the tasks that the team needs to do before the program is ready to launch? What are some of the things they need to keep in mind?

_____

_____

_____

_____

_____

_____

Have you ever been involved in the process of building a house? It's quite an experience. The basic structure—the foundation, the framing of the walls—happens pretty quickly. But the transformation of that framework into a finished home takes months. A friend who was in the middle of the process said, "It's amazing how many decisions we have to make every day—from where to put the electrical outlets to what kind of molding we want on the walls. I can hardly get my work done. I spend my days looking at faucets and doorknobs and light fixtures. I never realized how much work this project was going to involve, or how much time it was going to take!"

Developing a training program is a little like that, I think. It can involve a lot of work and take a lot of time to turn the design into a finished program. That's what you'll learn about in this chapter.

Here's some of what's covered in this chapter:

- The tasks involved in the development process
- Deciding whether to develop, adapt, or purchase the program
- Identifying and organizing the content
- Developing the learning activities
- Structuring the training program
- Developing the program materials
- Testing the program to make sure that everything works as planned
- Designing the evaluation that will be used to measure the program's success

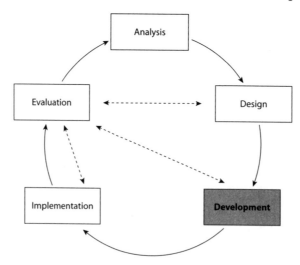

Rather than creating courses, you need to think of yourself as someone who is creating learning experiences.

Peter C. Honebein, Ph.D., "Creativity, Emergence, and the Design of Learning Experiences," in T.L. Gargiulo, A.M. Pangarkar, and T. Kirkwood (Eds.), *The Trainer's Portable Mentor*

1. What's Involved in Development

Check What You Know

Which statements about developing a training program are accurate?

1. ____ As long as you have paid enough attention to earlier stages of the instructional design process, it shouldn't take too long to develop the program.
2. ____ By the time you reach this stage of the process, you might already have selected some of the learning activities and developed a preliminary content outline.
3. ____ The order in which you do the development tasks is crucial.
4. ____ You might need to experiment until you find the best way of assembling the components of the program.

Developing a training program is arguably the most time-consuming part of the instructional design process. This is the stage in which you draw on everything you've done so far to create the program materials. Even if you are using—or considering—an off-the-shelf or preexisting program, an understanding of how training programs are developed will help you choose the right program. (See below for more on using off-the-shelf programs.)

The process of developing a training program includes these kinds of tasks:

- *Identifying and organizing the content*—the information, processes, procedures, and skills that the program needs to cover for the learners to be able to achieve the objectives. By the time you reach this stage, you'll already know a lot about the content from the process of analyzing the needs and developing the learning objectives; you might even have selected some of the learning activities and developed a preliminary content outline. Here, you will get right down to the details, decide what content learners need to achieve each of the learning objectives, and organize that content so the topics flow in a logical order that helps people learn.

- *Selecting or designing activities that help people learn the content.* You know from earlier chapters that the activities are the way in which you engage people and help them learn. As you develop the program, you'll seek a variety of activities that help people with different learning styles and preferences learn different types of content.

- *Organizing the program elements into a logical structure.* Training programs have lots of components. Sometimes they fall neatly into place, but if they do not, you might need to experiment until you find the best way of assembling them.

- *Developing or purchasing the program materials,* such as trainer guides, participant handouts or workbooks, games, software, props, videos, CD-ROMs—whatever the program requires.

- *Testing the program* on a representative sample of the audience and making whatever changes might be needed before rolling it out.

- *Designing the program evaluation*—the method or methods you will use to determine how well the program achieved the intended outcome.

The rest of this chapter provides details about those common tasks. As mentioned earlier, the order in which you do them usually doesn't matter much, nor does it matter whether you do all of them yourself, as long as each task gets done and receives sufficient attention.

How Long Does It Take to Develop a Training Program?

Every new instructional designer asks this question. But even those of us with years of experience can't really provide a satisfactory answer. The truth is, developing any training program takes the time it takes. For example, you can assume that even the simplest live, in-person workshop could take several days or even weeks to design and develop—perhaps as much as thirty to forty hours for each hour of classroom training.

The actual development time for a specific program depends on such factors as the topic, the objectives, the amount and types of content, the number and types of activities needed to achieve the objectives, the delivery system, the expertise of the people working on development, and more. After you've worked on a few programs, you'll start to get a sense of how much development time you'll need. And the best way to use that time efficiently is to make sure that you've paid enough attention to the earlier stages of the process—analysis and design—so that by the time you start developing materials, you know exactly what the program requires.

2. Develop, Adapt, or Purchase?

Check What You Know

Which of the statements about existing and off-the-shelf programs are accurate?

1. ___ Purchasing an off-the-shelf program is always a better option if your budget is limited.
2. ___ Even the best off-the-shelf programs seldom meet learners' needs as well as a program designed from scratch.

(Continued)

> 3. ___ One reason for using an existing or off-the-shelf program is that you do not have the expertise to develop a program on the topic.
> 4. ___ Existing or off-the-shelf programs can be good options when you need to get a training program up and running quickly.
> 5. ___ It can take more time to update and revise an existing program than to design and develop a new one.

Before we discuss the development process in detail, let's take a moment to talk about the use of existing or off-the-shelf programs. In some cases, you don't need to develop a program from scratch. Your organization might have a stockpile of existing programs that can be updated and adapted relatively easily, or you might be able to find an excellent, professionally developed off-the-shelf workshop or e-learning program that you can use as is or customize for your learners.

There are a number of circumstances under which you might consider an existing or off-the-shelf program, including these:

- Your time is limited—you need to get a program up and running quickly.

- You don't have the expertise to develop a program on the specific topic or to develop the type of program that would be best for the learners and the situation.

- There is an excellent program available that you can use with little or no customization.

When adapting existing programs or purchasing off-the-shelf programs, be careful not to try forcing a round peg into a square hole. It might take far more time to update and revise an existing program than to develop a new one. And no matter how well-designed it is, an off-the-shelf program might require too much customization to make it a practical way to achieve your goals.

To avoid wasting time, money, and effort on an existing or off-the-shelf program that really doesn't meet your needs, think about the following:

- Are the learning objectives consistent with those of your program? If the learning objectives of the program you are considering differ significantly from the ones that you've identified, the program is unlikely to achieve the desired outcome.

- Does the program meet the criteria for learner-centered, active training? Is it based on adult learning principles? Does it include activities that will engage learners and help them learn? Can you use the content and essential structure of the program but change activities so it is more involving?

- Is the program appropriate for your audience? Your type of organization? If not, what changes would need to be made to make it more relevant to your learners' real-life situations?

- How easy is the program to use? How much preparation will the trainer need? Some training programs require that trainers have a certain level of expertise, and some off-the-shelf programs require that trainers become certified.

- How much customizing does the program need? If it's an off-the shelf program, would you be allowed to make changes?

- How much time and money would you actually save by using an existing or off-the-shelf option instead of developing a program of your own?

At the end of this chapter, you'll find a worksheet that will help you decide whether to adapt an existing program, purchase an off-the-shelf program, or develop your own.

3. Identifying and Organizing the Content

As you put the design elements together, play with a variety of options . . . write down all the important topic-related concepts . . . on different pieces of paper or sticky notes . . . move pieces around, and figure out what goes together and what to let go of. . . . Remember to align every concept . . . with the learning outcomes of the training.

Sharon Bowman,
Training from the Back of the Room

Check What You Know

Suppose you are developing a training program to help team leaders conduct hiring interviews. What process would you use to decide what content is necessary for the program to achieve its objectives? Where would you begin?

_____

_____

_____

_____

_____

_____

Trainers have a tendency to include more content than can be covered in the time allowed, and usually far more than learners actually want or need. Chances are that by the time you reach the development stage, you have amassed far more content than you can actually use. Now you need to decide what content to include and what to leave out.

To pinpoint the essential content and keep yourself focused, start with the learning objectives. Go through them one at a time, asking, "What do people need to know or be able to do to achieve this objective?" Write down all the answers you come up with. This is a brainstorming process—ask the question over and over again and write down every answer.

Once you have generated a list of the topics to cover for each learning objective, you need to separate the wheat from the chaff—to figure out what's important, what doesn't need to be included, and what information is nice to know but not essential—and organize the content into a logical sequence of topics and subtopics.

Instructional designers have different ways of going about this process. Some use mind-mapping or other techniques that help them organize information visually. Some work on computers, others on flip-chart pages or whiteboards, and still others write content items on index cards or Post-it Notes so they can play around with different ways of organizing the information.

While you work, remember that ADDIE is not necessarily a linear process. As you gather more information, focus on what learners need to know, and think about what you can cover in the available time, you might find that you need to revise one or more of the learning objectives, and changes in learning objectives may dictate changes in the content.

How Long Will the Program Be?

At some point in the ADDIE process, you need to decide how long the program will be: Two hours? A full day? Two days? Ten hours over a four-week period? That question might already have been answered by the time you begin developing the program. For example, learners might only have a single day available for training. If so, you will need to limit the number of objectives to those that can successfully be covered in one day. If the time has not yet been set, you will determine how long the program needs to be during the development stage by estimating the time needed to achieve each of the learning objectives.

● ●

THINK ABOUT IT

For a training program on conducting hiring interviews, one of the learning objectives is, "Given a list of possible questions to ask during an interview, identify the questions that may

(Continued)

Training Fundamentals: Pfeiffer Essential Guides to Training Basics.
Copyright © 2010 by John Wiley & Sons, Inc.
Reproduced by permission of Pfeiffer, an Imprint of Wiley. www.Pfeiffer.com

legally be asked of job applicants." What are some of the things that a learner would need to know and/or be able to do to achieve this objective?

_____

_____

_____

_____

_____

_____

● ●

Here's an example of a process for identifying content that you can use as is or adapt to fit your own way of working.

1. Write one of the learning objectives at the top of a computer screen, a piece of paper, a whiteboard, or a flip-chart page. Divide the page into two columns. At the top of one column, write, "What learners already know." At the top of the other column, write, "What learners need to know." Then write down in one column or the other everything that occurs to you, without stopping to think about whether it's valid or a repeat of something you've already written, or anything else.

Example:

Objective: Prepare and distribute a meeting agenda that meets the criteria on a checklist.

What learners know/are able to do	What learners need to know/be able to do
What an agenda is	How to prepare an agenda
The purpose	Who should receive it
Why it's important	When it should be distributed
	The format
	How specific it should be
	How to prepare an agenda

Training Fundamentals: Pfeiffer Essential Guides to Training Basics.
Copyright © 2010 by John Wiley & Sons, Inc.
Reproduced by permission of Pfeiffer, an Imprint of Wiley. www.Pfeiffer.com

What learners know/are able to do	What learners need to know/be able to do
	What it should include
	How to handle last-minute changes
	How to gather information
	The purpose
	Who should contribute
	Estimating times
	What it should look like
	The components
	How to indicate responsibilities
	Using it during meetings
	Generating agenda items
	When meeting time is limited
	Breaks, openings, closings
	Choosing the place

2. Put question marks after any items on the "Already Know" and "Need to Know" lists that you're not sure about. (You might need to do some research to decide what to do with those items.) On the "Need to Know" list, cross out anything that is clearly not relevant or redundant, and put brackets around any items that are not essential.

Example:

What learners know/are able to do	What learners need to know/be able to do
What an agenda is	How to prepare an agenda
The purpose [?]	What it should include
Why it's important	Who should receive it
	When it should be distributed
	The format
	How specific it should be
	How to handle last-minute changes
	How to gather information
	The purpose [?]

(Continued)

What learners know/are able to do	What learners need to know/be able to do
	Who should contribute
	Estimating times
	~~What it should look like~~
	~~The components~~
	How to indicate responsibilities
	[Using it during meetings]
	Generating agenda items
	When meeting time is limited
	Breaks, openings, closings
	~~Choosing the place~~

3. Unless there is space to add more items on the "Need to Know" list, copy the items onto another computer screen, flip-chart page, sheet of paper, or document. Then read through the list again, asking the same old question: "What do learners need to know or be able to do to achieve the objective?" Add anything else that occurs to you, making sure that the added items are relevant and essential.

Example:

How to prepare an agenda

What it should include

Who should receive it

When it should be distributed

The format

How specific it should be

How to handle last-minute changes

How to gather information

The purpose

Who should contribute

Estimating times

How to indicate responsibilities

Generating agenda items

When meeting time is limited

Breaks, openings, closings

Building in flexibility

4. Group the items on the list into key topics and subtopics. One quick way to do that is to mark the first item on the list with an "A." Then go through the list quickly and mark any similar items with an "A." Once you reach the bottom of the list, start again, giving the second item a "B," and so on. If you're not sure about whether an item is more like "A" than "B" or "C," skip it or mark it with a question mark for the time being.

By this point, you will start to see topics emerging from your list. If the topic is already on the list, underline or circle it. If a group of items suggests a topic, write the topic and underline or circle it, giving it the same letter as the others in the group.

Example:

A	How to prepare an agenda		
A	What it should include		
B	Who should receive it		
B	When it should be distributed	B.	Distributing the agenda
C	The format for an agenda		
A	How specific it should be		
[?]	How to handle last-minute changes		
A	How to gather information		
D	The purpose of an agenda		
A	Who should contribute		
E	Estimating times for items	E	Estimating the time
A	How to indicate responsibilities		
A	Generating items		
[E?]	When meeting time is limited		
E	Breaks, openings, closings		
E	Building in flexibility		

5. List the topics and their subtopics, with the learning objective at the top. If an order suggests itself, put the topics in order as you copy them over. If an item in one category seems to belong in another, move it. Add any other topics that occur to you and delete any that seem redundant or unnecessary. When you're finished, you will have a rough outline of the content for that learning objective.

Example:

Objective: Prepare and distribute a meeting agenda that meets the criteria on a checklist.

1. The purpose of an agenda
2. Criteria for a useful agenda
3. The format for an agenda
   What an agenda should include
4. How to prepare an agenda
   Generating preliminary agenda items
   How to gather information for an agenda
   Who should contribute to an agenda
5. Estimating the time
   Estimating times for agenda items
   Breaks, openings, closings
   Limited meeting times
   Building in flexibility
6. Distributing the agenda
   Who should receive an agenda
   When the agenda should be distributed
7. How to handle last-minute changes

6. Repeat the process for each learning objective. Along the way, you may come up with topics that you're not sure what to do with. Collect these separately; when you've finished outlining the content for all the learning objectives, review the strays to decide where they belong—or whether they belong at all.

4. Developing Learning Activities

Most adults learn best when they are actively involved in their learning experiences. When learners discover concepts, rather than listen to them in a lecture . . . retention improves.

Jean Barbazette,
The Art of Great Training Delivery

Training Fundamentals: Pfeiffer Essential Guides to Training Basics.
Copyright © 2010 by John Wiley & Sons, Inc.
Reproduced by permission of Pfeiffer, an Imprint of Wiley. www.Pfeiffer.com

Check What You Know

Which type or types of activity might be best to accomplish each purpose?

(A) Lecture   (B) Small-group discussion   (C) Role play   (D) Game
(E) Simulation

1. ___ Help customer service managers draw on their own experience to develop strategies for meeting customers' needs.
2. ___ Let sales representatives try out techniques for closing a sale.
3. ___ Give new employees an overview of the organization's health benefits options.
4. ___ Help call center staff practice identifying the right answers to caller's questions.
5. ___ Help a management team learn to develop a mission and values statement and a strategic plan for a new company.

Learning activities are the instructional methods used to communicate the content and help people learn: lectures, discussions, demonstrations, debates, role plays, practice exercises, simulations, case studies, games, field trips, readings, assessments, interviews, peer teaching—the list goes on. As you already know, successful training programs use a variety of methods to encourage active participation, discovery, and collaborative learning, as well as to appeal to different learning styles and preferences.

The activities for a specific program depend on such factors as the objectives; the type of subject matter to be learned; the delivery method; the learners' characteristics and preferences; the time, equipment, facilities, and resources that are available; the trainer's expertise; and more. There is an overview of the different types in the table on pages 126 and 127. In this book, we focus on activities for workshops, but many of the same activities can be adapted to other delivery systems as well.

Types of Learning Activities

Type of Activity	Used to . . .	What to Consider	Examples
Lecture: One-way communication in which trainer delivers information to learners	Get a large amount of information across in a relatively short amount of time	Learners are passive, not active; keep lectures brief and use them sparingly; involve learners in some way (for example, ask questions); use visuals or props; follow with a discussion or experiential activity	Using visuals to support the presentation, trainer describes the organization's health benefits options, answers questions, and asks participants to use a worksheet to decide which option best meets their needs
Structured Discussions: Learners discuss a topic, usually in small groups, and summarize their discussion for the larger group	Help learners examine, analyze, explore a topic, express ideas, and share opinions; encourage them to draw on and share their knowledge and experience, and work together to solve problems	Highly interactive; can be time-consuming; may need careful facilitation to help groups stay on topic	Learners discuss their experiences as a customer and draw conclusions about what customers want
Demonstrations: The trainer and/or someone else shows learners how to do something; can be a live demonstration or a video	Show learners how to do a task, carry out a process, behave in a certain way, interact with others	Usually captures learners' interest; must be accurate and clearly presented enough for people to follow, and accompanied by necessary explanations; work best when immediately followed by opportunity to practice	Learners watch and listen while an expert goes through the process of assembling a piece of equipment, then try it themselves
Role Plays: Learners follow a script or instructions to act out a real or realistic situation	Help learners practice and experiment with new techniques; can provide insights into their own and other people's behaviors	Involve learners and help them learn by doing; take careful planning; can be time-consuming; some learners find role plays uncomfortable; work best when learners give and receive feedback and have a chance to reflect on their experience	A "manager" practices delegating a job to "an employee." The learners discuss what happened, then reverse roles and try it again
Case Studies: Learners read, analyze, and discuss a realistic situation, one that usually presents	Help people learn by discovery; encourage collaboration; help learners	Engaging and interactive; most learners find relevant cases engaging and interesting; some	Learners read a case about a company that struggled to compete in a difficult economic environment

a problem or shows the way people solved a problem	draw and share what they already know and apply what they are learning	people want to be given a black-and-white resolution to a problem; cases can be difficult to develop, and the activity can take a lot of time	and succeeded, pull out the lessons, and determine the implications of what they learned for their own organizations
Questionnaires and Assessments: Learners answer questions or complete a rating instrument that helps them evaluate their knowledge, skills, and attitudes; may include comparison with observers' responses to same question	Help learners understand and reflect on their personal relationship to what they are learning and determine what they may need to improve or change	Most learners like these types of assessments, although some find them uncomfortable; questions or instrument needs to be carefully designed and accompanied by careful facilitation; learners need to do something with the feedback	Managers complete a questionnaire to identify their management styles, share the results with a partner or a small group, reflect on the implications, and develop an action plan for making changes to become a better manager
Games: Learners compete with one another (or with themselves) to answer questions or perform tasks; involve rules and may include rewards for winners	Help learners learn facts, practice tasks, solve problems, come up with new ideas, review and reinforce what they have learned	Fun, engaging way of learning that can be done in a group or individually (learners play against themselves); game must be carefully designed to achieve a specific purpose; some learners find games "silly"	Variation of "Concentration": learners look for matching pairs in a deck of cards. Learners compete in teams to come up with the most correct answers to a question in the least amount of time
Practice Exercises: Learners practice doing what they have learned and get feedback	Help learners learn by doing—try out new learning, experiment, and make adjustments	Engaging; can be done individually or with others; helps learners prepare to apply learning to the real world	After learning a process for planning, organizing, and writing reports that meet specific criteria, learners plan and write a report of their own, getting feedback from one another and/or the trainer
Simulations: Activities that attempt to provide a realistic real-world experience	Help learners apply the learning in a situation that closely approximates their real world	Can be very engaging and involving; helps learners apply learning to their real world; can be time-consuming and costly	Learners come up with a mission, values, and a strategic plan for a fictional company

Here are some steps you can take to choose relevant activities that meet the needs of the learners and the situation.

● *Review the learning objectives and the content outline.* For each topic or subtopic, think about what people need to learn. Do they need to acquire knowledge? Learn new skills? Change their attitudes? Does what they need to learn require analyzing and thinking? Understanding concepts or how something works? Memorizing facts? Follow specific steps? Perform certain actions?

● *Think about the learners.* What's their preferred learning style? What kinds of activities would they be comfortable with? What kinds of activities might make them uncomfortable or resistant?

● *Consider the time, equipment, facilities, and expertise that are available.* Some games, simulations, and experiential activities can require a significant amount of time, special equipment or facilities, and special expertise, while others, such as interactive lectures and group discussions, can be adjusted to fit the available time and resources.

● *Consider the size and characteristics of the group.* Some activities are hard to do with large groups, especially those in which learners practice doing something and get feedback from their colleagues. For example, the group for a workshop on making presentations would need to be limited in size so that everyone would have a chance to practice and receive feedback. Discussions are harder to manage in very large groups. Also, some activities work best when learners have approximately the same levels of experience and prior knowledge and when they are at similar levels of the organization. For example, in a workshop on management techniques, it can be difficult to

> ## Guidelines for Selecting Learning Activities
>
> - Review the learning objectives and the content that needs to be covered.
> - Think about the learners' styles and preferences.
> - Consider the time, equipment, facilities, and expertise that are available.
> - Consider the size and characteristics of the group.
> - Consider the cost.

meet everyone's needs if some participants have been managers for years while others have just begun preparing for a management role.

- *Consider the cost.* Activities that require custom-written software or custom-produced video, certified trainers, special equipment and facilities, expensive materials, or user fees might be too expensive for your budget, even though they might be the best way for people to learn.

Experiential Learning

Check What You Know

Which statement most accurately describes "experiential learning" as the term is most commonly used in training?

1. ____ The practice exercises that help learners apply what they learn.
2. ____ A process for helping people learn through discovery.
3. ____ On-the-job training with the use of job aids.

Many of the most useful learning experiences follow some form of what is commonly called experiential learning, a powerful process that draws on adult learning principles to help people learn through discovery. Although the models differ, experiential learning activities commonly have five key steps: experiencing, sharing, processing, generalizing, and applying. The learners participate in an activity; reflect on what happened and, usually, share their reactions and observations with others; examine and interpret what happened; make a connection between the experience and the real world; and use or decide how to use what they have learned.

Training Fundamentals: Pfeiffer Essential Guides to Training Basics.
Copyright © 2010 by John Wiley & Sons, Inc.
Reproduced by permission of Pfeiffer, an Imprint of Wiley. www.Pfeiffer.com

No matter how often this model is adapted, the essential phases are usually the same. Here's how this process might work in an interviewing workshop.

1. *Experiencing*—With little or no guidance from the trainer, learners participate in an activity that involves doing something, such as discussing a topic, solving a problem, playing a game, completing an assessment, doing a role play, or taking part in a simulation.

   Example: Learners do a role play in which they interview one another for a position.

2. *Reflecting and Sharing*—The learners think about what happened during the activity, answering such questions as "How did you feel about . . . ?" "What happened when . . . ?" "What did you see/hear . . . ?" "What was the most difficult? The easiest?" If the experiential learning activity is being done in a group, which is usually the case, the learners share their reactions and observations with others.

   Example: After the interview role play, learners meet in small groups to discuss what happened in what worked and what didn't, what was easy and what was hard. Each small group summarizes its discussions for the rest of the participants.

   > Not all experiential learning models have five distinct steps. For example, in *Creative Training Techniques*, Bob Pike presents a simplified version that he calls the ADA Approach: learners do an Activity, Discuss what went on, and decide how the learning can be Applied in the real world. What's important is to start with the activity and then help learners think about and apply what they've learned.

3. *Processing (also called Conceptualizing)*—Learners make sense out of the experience by exploring and analyzing what happened and looking for themes and patterns. They answer such questions as, "What did you learn about . . . ?" "How does what you learned relate to . . . "? "What patterns do you see in . . . ?" "What similar experiences have you had?"

   Example: Back in their small groups, learners discuss what they learned about interviewing from the activity and share the patterns and themes that emerged with the larger group.

4. *Generalizing (also called Connecting)*—Learners relate the experience to what they already know and have experienced to find general trends, common truths, and real-life principles. They might answer these kinds of questions: "What did you learn about yourself?" "How does this experience help you understand . . . ?" "How does this experience relate to . . . ?" "Why is it important to . . . ?"

Example: The trainer asks questions to help learners focus on how what they learned about interviewing relates to interviews they have conducted and experienced.

5. *Applying*—Learners examine how they can use the learning in the real world and make commitments to take specific actions. The questions include, "What actions will you take to use . . . ?" "What changes will you make in . . . ?" "What will you do differently the next time that . . . ?"

Example: The trainer asks participants to decide what they will do differently when they conduct interviews and then repeat the role play activity, using the new learning.

5. Structuring the Training Program

Check What You Know

Which of the following statements about structuring a training program are accurate?

1. ____ The learning objectives often determine the sequence.
2. ____ To engage workshop participants more quickly, use a challenging activity such as a role play within the first hour.
3. ____ If you are short on time, it's okay to omit one or more of the breaks.

As you go through the process of identifying the content to include and selecting activities to use, you are likely to come up with at least a preliminary program structure in which the component parts are arranged into a logical sequence. Your goal is to find a sequence in which each topic and activity builds on what's come before and forms the foundation for what is to come next. You will need to develop a workshop opening that engages learners, stimulates their interest, and helps them become comfortable with you and one another; you will also need a closing that helps people review the key learning points, decide what they will do to use what they've learned, and think about how they can continue the learning process. The timing and pacing of the topics and activities should help learners stay focused and engaged.

Here are some things to think about when you decide how to structure the program:

- The learning objectives often determine the sequence. If you haven't already done so, arrange the learning objectives in what seems to be the most logical order, and then organize the topics and activities into a logical order for each learning objective. If you have trouble deciding whether one objective, or one topic or activity, should come before another, ask: "What do learners need to know before they can understand/recognize/ do XYZ?"

- If you plan to use activities that might take some learners out of their comfort zones, make sure that they are preceded by activities that help learners trust you and one another. For example, wait until people feel comfortable in the learning environment before asking them to do role plays or discuss sensitive issues.

- Once you have established the sequence, plan introductions that tell people where they are going, summaries that remind them of where they have been, and transitions that form a bridge from one segment of the program to the next.

- Check the timing and pacing carefully. Make sure that all the activities, including the time needed to introduce them and to summarize the key learning points, fit into the time you have

Creating the Sequence

Here are some of the options for arranging topics and activities:

- Order of priority
- Familiar to unfamiliar
- Easy to difficult
- Logical order
- General to specific
- Comfortable to risky
- Simple to complex

available. Vary the activities and the ways in which content is presented so that the program does not fall into a hum-drum rhythm. Consider when to take breaks, and be careful not to omit breaks because you are short on time. Think about the times of day when people are most likely to have trouble focusing; you might want to schedule a lively activity during the period after lunch when people feel like putting their heads down on their desks for a nap.

What a Workshop Opening Should Do

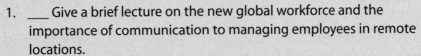

Check What You Know

Which of the following would be the most effective way to open a workshop on managing remotely?

1. ____ Give a brief lecture on the new global workforce and the importance of communication to managing employees in remote locations.
2. ____ Show slides with the workshop objectives and the agenda and ask whether participants have questions.
3. ____ Ask participants to introduce themselves to the others at their tables and share an experience they have had with remote management, either as a manager or an employee.

What happens during the first few minutes of a workshop can significantly affect people's ability to learn. The opening of a workshop plays a vital role in capturing learners' attention, letting them know what to expect, and helping them understand why the training is worth their time.

The opening activities should accomplish the following:

- Help learners feel comfortable with the trainer and with one another
- Get people participating actively
- Establish the expectation that this is a learner-centered, not a trainer-centered, workshop
- Provide essential information about why the workshop is being held and what people are going to learn
- Help participants see how they and their organizations will benefit from the training
- Let people know what they will accomplish (the learning objectives)
- Give people a preview of the workshop (the agenda)
- Provide any logistical information people need (location of restrooms, where lunch will be served, how to get parking tickets validated)
- Establish ground rules or norms (cell phones off, come back on time from breaks, listen while others are talking, keep confidential information confidential)

What a Workshop Closing Should Do

Just as the opening of a workshop prepares people to learn, the closing prepares them to take what they have learned back to their workplace. The closing is where people pull together what they've learned, think about how they can use the learning, and decide what they will do next.

At a minimum, the closing activities should accomplish the following:

- Provide an opportunity for participants to review the key learning points and think about what will be most useful to them
- Help learners decide how they will use what they have learned
- Increase the likelihood that people will use the learning by asking them to commit to specific actions
- Give learners feel a sense of accomplishment
- Help people determine what they can do to continue learning

6. Preparing the Agenda

Once you've developed the workshop structure, you're ready to prepare an agenda that includes an overview of the topics, the sequence in which they'll be covered, and the timing. The agenda serves as a working outline for developing program materials. It helps you make sure that everything "flows" smoothly and the topics and activities are clearly linked to the learning objectives. Identifying start and stop times for each activity helps you determine how long the workshop will be and see whether you need to make changes to fit into the available time.

Here's an example of the first part of an agenda.

Times	Topics and Activities	Training AIDS
9:00 – 9:30	**Opening**	**Slide: Welcome**
1._____	Introduce myself and give purpose of workshop (brief)	Slide: Purpose
2._____	Activity 1: Introductions and opening question (10 minutes)	
3._____	Activity 2: Expectations and objectives (5 minutes)	Slide: Objectives
4._____	Review agenda	Slide: Agenda
5._____	Explain logistics	
6._____	Establish ground rules and set up a parking lot	Flip chart
7._____	Make a transition to the next segment	

Below is a process you can follow to prepare an agenda. You may not need to do all the steps or follow them in the order shown. After you develop the workshop materials, you will revise this agenda into an at-a-glance agenda you can use during the workshop and one that you can send out to participants.

1. List the topics and activities in order and "group" them into workshop segments.

2. Indicate transitions between topics, activities, and segments.

3. Write a brief description of the purpose for each segment and each activity within a segment. Except for the opening and the closing, the purpose should be clearly linked to a specific learning or enabling objective.

4. Estimate start/stop times for each segment, activity, and break (including lunch).

7. Developing Program Materials

When contractors take on the job of building a house, they examine the plans to figure out what materials they will need—what kind of lumber, how much concrete, how much copper pipe. Nearly everything needs to be purchased or fabricated—or at least ordered—before construction can get underway.

It's the same with constructing a training program. Once you have identified the delivery method, content, and activities, and developed the structure, you need to develop, adapt, collect, purchase, and fabricate everything needed to put the program together. For some programs, the materials might include only a few handouts and slides, the agenda, and some trainer notes; others might require a complete trainer's guide and participant workbook, a PowerPoint presentation, DVDs, assessment instruments, computer software, and more.

This chart shows examples of the kinds of materials you commonly need for various types of training programs.

Live workshop	Facilitator's guide or trainer notes
	Participant workbook and/or handouts
	PowerPoint slides
	Posters
	Props
	Audiotapes and/or DVDs
	Assessments
	Games
	Rosters, evaluation forms
Virtual workshop	Facilitator's guide or instructor notes
	Slides, screen shots, documents
	Participant handouts and/or reference material
Self-paced print program	Trainer or administrator's guide or notes
	Self-paced workbooks
Self-paced e-learning program	Trainer or administrator's guide or notes
	e-Learning software (downloadable or CD-ROM)
	Reference material
Podcast	Podcast script
	Podcast (downloadable or CD)
Video	Video script
	Video (downloadable or DVD)
	(possibly) Trainer's guide with discussion questions

Training Fundamentals: Pfeiffer Essential Guides to Training Basics.
Copyright © 2010 by John Wiley & Sons, Inc.
Reproduced by permission of Pfeiffer, an Imprint of Wiley. www.Pfeiffer.com

Developing and obtaining everything the program requires can be—and often is—the most time-consuming part of the entire process. To make sure it goes smoothly, you'll need a project plan that includes:

- What needs to be done—details of all the tasks that need to be accomplished
- Responsibilities—who will be responsible for which tasks
- Timelines—when each task must be completed

There's a Training Materials Work Plan template on page 156 at the end of the chapter that you can use as is or adapt to fit your own situation.

These guidelines can help you use development time and resources efficiently:

- *Leave enough time.* Even a simple half-day workshop can take weeks to develop, and it can take months to develop an e-learning program. If you are adapting an existing program, remember that it can take as much time to customize a program as to develop a new one.

- *Think about who will deliver the training.* Trainers who are involved in a workshop design and development process might need only an agenda and a few notes, while those who are not already familiar with the topic and the program may need a detailed script. Subject-matter experts and managers who deliver training may need guidelines to help them prepare for and conduct the workshop. Trainers and others who deliver print self-study and e-learning programs need instructions and guidelines to help them plan, prepare for, administer, and follow up the training.

- *Keep materials simple, lean, professional, and easy to use.* If a trainer's guide or participant workbook that you are developing begins to resemble one of those huge binders that homeowners' associations hand out, stop. Keep the writing to a minimum. Use formatting devices and graphics to make materials easy to read. Make sure that materials present a professional image; sloppy, error-filled handouts, workbooks, slides, or e-learning screens indicate sloppy, error-filled thinking and convey little respect for the learner.

- *Develop materials with revision in mind.* Things change, and there's a very good chance—almost a certainty in many situations—that you or someone else will need to add, delete, or rearrange content and activities at some point. That's hard to do if the materials have been printed and bound like this book. As you develop and package training materials, think about how you can make it easy and inexpensive to incorporate revisions.

Helpful Handouts

Handouts can reinforce and support learning, or they can be distracting and annoying. Here are some suggestions for making sure that the materials you give out to the participants help rather than hinder the learning process.

- Single sheets of paper or stapled packets end up scattered on the tables or the floor. Organize handouts into a folder or a binder, or put them into a spiral-bound workbook. Include a table of contents and tabs, if necessary, to help learners find specific pages easily. And be sure to number the pages.
- Avoid overwhelming learners with too much "nice-to-know" information. Make sure that each handout serves a specific purpose. It's fine to include some relevant supplementary information for use after the workshop, but hand it out at the end of the training, put it at the end of the workbook, send it electronically, or make it available on a website.
- Make handouts easy to read and use. Avoid long paragraphs of text—use bullet points instead. Leave lots of room for notes. If you use photographs, photocopies, or screen shots, make sure they are crisp and clear. Start a new page when the topic shifts or a new activity begins.
- Pay attention to the quality of materials. Handouts should be consistent in format and have a clean, neat, professional look. You can use graphics to liven up materials as long as the graphics are appropriate and do not just add clutter to the pages. Proofread carefully to catch any errors.

Training Fundamentals: Pfeiffer Essential Guides to Training Basics.
Copyright © 2010 by John Wiley & Sons, Inc.
Reproduced by permission of Pfeiffer, an Imprint of Wiley. www.Pfeiffer.com

What's a Trainer's Guide?

A trainer's guide, or facilitator's guide, is a document that guides a trainer through the process of delivering a workshop. It is usually written so that someone who was not involved in the design process and may not be very familiar with the subject matter of the training can set up, prepare for, and conduct training.

The contents and level of detail in a trainer's guide depend on the subject matter, the experience, and the expertise of the people who will be delivering the training. For inexperienced trainers who are unfamiliar with the subject matter, a comprehensive trainer's guide might include:

- A description of the program and the target audience
- The learning objectives
- Background information about the subject
- Guidelines and checklists for planning, preparing for, and conducting training
- An at-a-glance agenda
- A detailed script that clearly lays out what the trainer should say and do at each point in the workshop
- Guidelines for following up training
- An electronic version and printouts of the slides
- Instructions for activities, including pre-work assignments
- Supplemental information, including answers to frequently asked questions
- A reading/resource list

What Are Trainer Notes?

Less comprehensive than a facilitator's guide, trainer notes are most commonly put together for and used by a trainer who is already familiar with the training program. They can be as simple as a printout of the agenda with handwritten notes or printouts of the slides with Notes pages, or as complex as a detailed outline that includes estimated times, key learning points, activity instructions, and visual aids for each segment of a workshop.

8. Testing the Program

Check What You Know

Which is the most effective way to make sure that a training program works as expected?

1. ___ Ask an experienced trainer to review all the program materials.
2. ___ Try it out with a representative sample of the target audience.
3. ___ Walk through it with a colleague or two.

Companies routinely test new products before sending them out to the market—they want to be sure that a product works the way it is supposed to work and meets the need it is supposed to fill. Even the most experienced training professionals cannot know for sure how well a training program is going to work until they have tested it by trying it out with a representative sample of the target audience. Trainers call this process "running a pilot" or "validating" the training program design. (Some trainers refer to the pilot as a "beta," borrowing from the process used to test a new software program.)

A pilot gives you valuable information about how well the program works. In particular, you can learn:

- How well the activities work to engage people and help them learn
- How long everything takes
- Whether any instructions are unclear
- Whether any content is missing
- Whether there is enough variety to maintain participants' interest and keep them focused
- Whether anything is in the wrong place
- Whether breaks fall at inconvenient times

Running a pilot takes time and resources, which is the reason that many instructional designers skip this step or truncate it severely. But the savings from not trying out the program are usually illusory. There are costs to training programs that don't work well, too, including the money spent producing materials, participants' time, the costs of facilities and equipment, and administrative expenses. There are also the hidden costs—frustrated expectations, loss of credibility, unmet goals. So even if you are unable to run a full-scale test, look for a way to try out key components of the program with a few representative participants.

For a pilot to achieve its objective of letting you know what works and what needs to be changed, follow these guidelines:

- Make sure that the participants are as representative as possible of the learners for whom the program was designed. Ideally, they should have about the same level of prior knowledge or skills and the same need for the information. Testing a workshop on accounting practices with a group of training associates or customer service representatives may not give you valid results.

- If possible, run the entire program, as it was designed. Do all the activities. If the program includes pre-work, ask the test group to do it. If you are using an assessment instrument, use it. Treat the pilot as a full-scale dress rehearsal, not simply a run-through.

- If necessary, try out segments of the program before the full-scale pilot. If you are using a complicated activity, for example, pull together a few people and take them through it during the design process. Then you can make adjustments in the activity—or replace it—before the pilot and use the pilot to make sure that the revised version works.

- Use draft materials. You don't have to spend time and money producing final materials with high-level graphics for a pilot. In most cases, final drafts work just fine, as long as they are clear and easy to use.

- Ask an experienced training professional to sit in on the pilot and give you (or the trainer) feedback. That person will be able to notice things that are not apparent to the person running the program.

9. Designing the Program Evaluation

Check What You Know

Francesca is nearly ready to launch the customer service representative workshop. First, she needs to design the program evaluation. What are some of the ways for evaluating the success of her program?

_____

_____

_____

_____

If you watch old black-and-white movies, you've probably seen several that included a scene showing the producers, the director, and the cast waiting anxiously for the newspapers with the opening-night reviews of a Broadway show. Will it be a hit? Or has everyone's hard work—and the investors' money—resulted in a flop?

The process of evaluating a training program is more complicated than the process of reviewing a Broadway show, but the purpose is similar: to find out whether the program was a success—how well it met its objectives, whether it needs to be improved, and what value it provides in return for the organization's investment. Yet although the evaluation stage of ADDIE is, like the analysis stage, one of the most important, it is also one of the most neglected. That's because a full-scale evaluation can take a great deal of time, attention, and expertise. Thus, the decision about how thoroughly to evaluate a given training program depends on how critical the training is to the organization, how many times the program will be repeated, the size of the investment in the program, and other factors.

Training Fundamentals: Pfeiffer Essential Guides to Training Basics.
Copyright © 2010 by John Wiley & Sons, Inc.
Reproduced by permission of Pfeiffer, an Imprint of Wiley. www.Pfeiffer.com

But wait—why are we talking about the evaluation now, before the program has been implemented? Good question! It's because, even though the actual evaluation takes place after the program, it needs to be designed much earlier. In fact, planning the evaluation starts with writing the learning objectives that specify what people will be able to do as a result of training. The basis for evaluating program success is established earlier when the training needs are identified, the learning objectives developed, and the criteria for measuring program success established.

The key questions that trainers and their organization face are what to evaluate and how to evaluate. First, they need to identify the questions they want the evaluation to answer: Did the participants find the program interesting and enjoyable? What did participants learn? Did participants achieve the learning objectives? Has training made a real change in people's performance, behavior, or attitudes? Did the program meet the organization's business goals? This kind of information not only helps organizations and trainers improve existing programs, but it helps them develop more effective training in the future.

Different Levels of Evaluation

Although there are different methodologies for evaluating training success, the most commonly used is some version of Donald Kirkpatrick's Four Levels of Evaluation, described in his well-known book, *Evaluating Training Programs*, now in its third edition. If you've ever attended a workshop, you are familiar with the first level, the questionnaire or discussion that comes at the end, asking how well you thought the program went.

Level 1 evaluations, often called "smile sheets" because participants, not waiting to hurt the trainer's feelings, often focus on the positive and hesitate to mention what they didn't like, are easy to administer and provide immediate feedback, so many training programs are never evaluated in any other way. "Smile sheets" do provide useful information about what's working and what could be improved. But they are only the first step in the evaluation process. The other levels, which require more time and effort, provide vital information about what participants learned, the degree to which they are applying what they learned, and the impact of the program on the organization.

Whether or not you are directly involved in any evaluations beyond Level 1, it's helpful to have some understanding of the different levels, so let's take a closer look.

Level 1: Participants' Reaction to Training

Level 1 evaluations are intended to answer the question, "How satisfied were participants with their training experience?" The information is most commonly gathered by asking participants to fill out a questionnaire or an electronic survey (the "smile sheet") at the end of the program, but sometimes it is gathered in an informal discussion ("What worked? What didn't?") or by conducting interviews with participants shortly after the program has been completed. When the right questions are asked, Level 1 evaluations provide important information: How well do participants feel the program met their needs? How effective was the trainer? How well did the activities help them learn? Did any time seem to be wasted? Any information or activities appear to be unnecessary? Anything missing? What changes might improve the program?

But the usefulness of Level 1 evaluations is very limited. They are subjective, and it can be difficult to separate the participants' level of satisfaction with the trainer's style and personality from their satisfaction with the program itself. In fact, participants who like the trainer may refrain from making negative comments because they don't want to hurt the person's feelings.

Level 2: Participants' Learning

This level helps trainers determine the extent to which learners have actually changed their attitudes, gained new knowledge, and/or gained new skills—in other words, how well they have achieved the learning objectives. Methods for evaluating learning include written or performance tests or assessments, surveys, observation, and interviews.

Level 2 evaluations are useful in determining what participants have learned, but they also have their limitations. There needs to be a standard against which to measure change or improvement—in other words, you need to know what people knew or could do, or what their attitudes were before training. It can be difficult, time-consuming, and costly to develop tests, assessments, or interview questions that provide valid results, and although observing people perform in a real or simulated situation provides useful information about what they are able to do or the way in which they behave, observation is necessarily subjective and can require a great deal of time.

Level 3: Participants' Behavior

Remember that the primary purpose of training is to change or improve performance in the workplace. This level of evaluation measures how well participants are applying what they learned. For most training programs, it is a far more valid evaluation method, but it can be difficult and costly to do. Methodologies include directly observing on-the-job performance or the results of performance; interviews with managers, colleagues, customers, and others; and/or surveys. Unlike Level 1 and Level 2 evaluations, which can be done immediately after training has been completed, Level 3 evaluations can be done only after the participants have had the time—and opportunity—to apply what they learned.

Level 3 evaluations are also complicated by the fact that it can be difficult to identify the reasons that participants have or have not successfully changed or improved their performance. For example, they might have improved because something in the environment improved; they might not have improved because they have not had opportunities to apply what they learned, their managers are unsupportive of a change in behavior, they do not have necessary equipment, or changes in organizational structure or procedures mean they no longer need to use what they learned.

> ## Kirkpatrick's Four Levels of Evaluation
>
> Level 1: How satisfied were the participants?
> Level 2: How much did participants learn?
> Level 3: What change in behavior occurred as a result of the program?
> Level 4: What were the results of training?

Level 4: Results of Training

As organizations increasingly examine the value of every activity, they are increasingly examining the impact of training on business results. Level 4 evaluations measure the degree to which the training actually achieved the desired results—the desired outcome identified in the needs assessment.

One reason why Level 4 evaluations are seldom done is that that question can be very difficult to answer. It's difficult to collect information—even to determine what information should be gathered. There is seldom a clear baseline against which to compare the results; and it's usually very hard to separate out which results—or lack of results—were due to training and which to other factors.

The Fifth Level of Evaluation: ROI

Some people interpret the fourth level of Kirkpatrick's model as measuring the organization's return on investment (ROI) from a training program. But author and researcher Dr. Jack Phillips describes a fifth level that directly addresses the impact of training on business results—specific business goals and objectives. Fifth-level evaluations ask, in essence, "Were the benefits of this training worth the cost?" The difficulty, of course, is in assessing those costs and the ROI with any amount of accuracy. As with some of the other levels of evaluation, it can be extremely difficult to distinguish the ways in which training actually contributed to the results. For more information, visit www.roiinstitute.net.

Quick Quiz

List the three to five key learning points from this chapter that will be most helpful to you.

_____

_____

_____

_____

_____

What's Next?

Your training program is finished and ready to go. Now it's time to bring the program to the learners. You'll learn about how to do that in the next chapter.

Apply What You Learn

Do the following for your training program.

1. Decide whether you will develop the program from scratch, adapt an existing program, or purchase an off-the-shelf program. If you plan to adapt an existing program or purchase an off-the-shelf program, where will you find it and what kinds of changes will you need to make?
2. For each learning objective, select the content to include and the activities that you will use to help people learn.
3. Prepare a preliminary agenda that shows the sequence of activities and estimated times for each activity.
4. Prepare a project plan for developing materials.
5. Decide how you can test the program to make sure that everything works as planned and identify changes that need to be made before the program is launched.
6. Decide what you, the trainer, and/or others will do to evaluate the success of training.

Answers to Exercises

Check What You Know

Which statements about developing a training program are accurate?

1. ___ As long as you have paid enough attention to earlier stages of the instructional design process, it shouldn't take too long to develop the program.
2. _X_ By the time you reach this stage of the process, you might already have selected some of the learning activities and developed a preliminary content outline.
3. ___ The order in which you do the development tasks is crucial.
4. _X_ You might need to experiment until you find the best way of assembling the components of the program.

Check What You Know

Which of the statements about existing and off-the-shelf programs are accurate?

1. ____ Purchasing an off-the-shelf program is always a better option if your budget is limited.
2. ____ Even the best off-the-shelf programs seldom meet learners' needs as well as a program designed from scratch.
3. _X_ One reason for using an existing or off-the-shelf program is that you do not have the expertise to develop a program on the topic.
4. _X_ Existing or off-the-shelf programs can be good options when you need to get a training program up and running quickly.
5. _X_ It can take more time to update and revise an existing program than to design and develop a new one.

THINK ABOUT IT

For a training program on conducting hiring interviews, one of the learning objectives is, "Given a list of possible questions to ask during an interview, identify the questions that may legally be asked of job applicants." What are some of the things that a learner would need to know and/or be able to do to achieve this objective?

Two of the things learners would need to know are what laws and regulations apply to the questions asked of job applicants and what questions may not legally be asked. Learners might also need to know how to use a job aid to help them avoid illegal questions and what to do if an applicant volunteers information on a topic that cannot be legally addressed. (Your responses might differ.)

Check What You Know

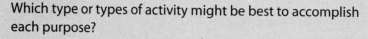

Which type or types of activity might be best to accomplish each purpose?

(A) Lecture   (B) Small-group discussion   (C) Role play
(D) Game   (E) Simulation

1. B, C, E   Help customer service managers draw on their own experience to develop strategies for meeting customers' needs.
2. C, D, E   Let sales representatives try out techniques for closing a sale.
3. A   Give new employees an overview of the organization's health benefits options.
4. C, D, E   Help call center staff practice identifying the right answers to caller's questions.
5. B, E   Help a management team learn to develop a mission and values statement and a strategic plan for a new company.

Check What You Know

Which statement most accurately describes "experiential learning" as the term is most commonly used in training?

1. ___ The practice exercises that help learners apply what they learn.
2. _X_ A process for helping people learn through discovery.
3. ___ On-the-job training with the use of job aids

Check What You Know

Which of the following statements about structuring a training program are accurate?

1. _X_ The learning objectives often determine the sequence.
2. ___ To engage workshop participants more quickly, use a challenging activity such as a role play within the first hour.
3. ___ If you are short on time, it's okay to omit one or more of the breaks.

Check What You Know

Which of the following would be the most effective way to open a workshop on managing remotely?

1. ___ Give a brief lecture on the new global workforce and the importance of communication to managing employees in remote locations.
2. ___ Show slides with the workshop objectives and the agenda and ask whether participants have questions.
3. _ X_ Ask participants to introduce themselves to the others at their tables and share an experience they have had with remote management, either as a manager or an employee.

Check What You Know

Which is the most effective way to make sure that a training program works as expected?

1. ___ Ask an experienced trainer to review all the program materials.
2. _X_ Try it out with a representative sample of the target audience.
3. ___ Walk through it with a colleague or two.

Worksheet

Worksheet: Adapt, Purchase, or Develop?

Use this checklist to help you decide whether to adapt an existing program, purchase an off-the-shelf program, or develop your own program.

Topic: ______________________________

Target audience: ______________________________

Delivery method: ______________________________

Program you are considering: ______________________________

- ❑ The content and instructional approach are appropriate and relevant for the target audience.

  Notes:

  ____

  ____

- ❑ The content is appropriate and relevant for the organization.

  Notes:

  ____

  ____

- ❑ The program includes the right amount of content.

  Notes:

  ____

  ____

❑ The content is accurate and complete.

Notes:

_____

_____

❑ The learning objectives accurately reflect what participants in this program need to accomplish.

Notes:

_____

_____

❑ The instructional approach meets the criteria for learner-centered, active training.

Notes:

_____

_____

❑ The instructional approach is based on adult learning principles.

Notes:

_____

_____

❑ The program includes activities that will engage learners and help them learn.

Notes:

_____

_____

❏ There is enough variety to appeal to different learning styles and preferences.

Notes:

_____

_____

❏ The activities can be easily revised to be more relevant to learners' real-life situations and to increase learner involvement without compromising the program's essential content and structure.

Notes:

_____

_____

❏ The program has all the necessary components.

Notes:

_____

_____

❏ The program is easy to use.

Notes:

_____

_____

❏ The trainer needs no special expertise or certifications to deliver this program.

Notes:

_____

_____

(Continued)

❑ Using this program would save a significant amount of time and money.

Notes:

_____

_____

❑ Other considerations:

_____

_____

_____

_____

_____

_____

_____

_____

_____

_____

_____

_____

_____

_____

_____

_____

_____

_____

_____

_____

Training Materials Work Plan Template

Material(s)	Source	Responsibility	Deadline	Notes

Material(s)	Source	Responsibility	Deadline	Notes

6

Implementing Training Programs

The first time I traveled abroad, I seriously underestimated how much work it would be to get ready—making plane reservations, finding places to stay, wrapping up my work projects, getting someone to water my plants, not to mention packing. By the time I settled into my airline seat, I was exhausted. It turned out to be a great trip. But as I thought back on it after I got home, I realized that I would have enjoyed it more if I'd given myself more time to prepare. And if I hadn't left everything until the last minute, I would have brought fewer things, made better use of the time, and spent my money more wisely. I had learned some things about traveling that I could use to make future trips more enjoyable.

Some of those lessons apply to the process of delivering a training program. There's a lot to do to get ready. It's easy to underestimate the time you'll need, and if you do, you are likely to find yourself rushing around at the last minute and exhausted by the time the workshop begins. In this chapter, you'll learn about what you need to do to prepare so that you are ready and relaxed when participants arrive. You'll also learn how to deliver training in a way that helps people achieve the learning objectives.

Here's an overview of what you'll find in this chapter:

- What needs to be done before a workshop
- Scheduling the training
- Notifying participants and preparing them to learn
- Setting up and maintaining an environment that is conducive to learning
- Confirming the arrangements and making contingency plans
- Getting a workshop started
- Helping the workshop stay on track and run smoothly
- Managing the learning group

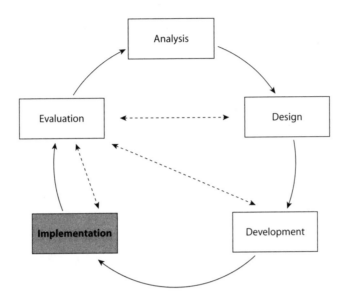

Implementation Stage of the ADDIE Model

Whenever I stand in front of a group, I remind myself that the collective knowledge and experience of it is far greater than my own.

Terrence L. Gargiulo and Robb Murray, "Some Basics from a Couple of Training Pros," in T.L. Gargiulo, A.M. Pangarkar, and T. Kirkwood (Eds.), *The Trainer's Portable Mentor*

You—or an instructional design team—have designed and developed a great program, tested and revised it, and produced the final materials. Now the program is ready to launch. That's the implementation stage of the ADDIE process, shown in the model, and for training to be successful, it requires as much care and attention as the earlier stages.

There are two parts to the process of implementing a training program: what you do before training begins, and what you do during the training itself. Workshops take the most planning and preparation, so we'll focus on them here. Many of these tasks, such as notifying and preparing participants, are necessary for implementing other types of training as well.

1. Before the Workshop

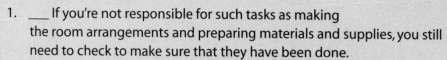

Check What You Know

Which of the following statements do you think are valid?

1. ____ If you're not responsible for such tasks as making the room arrangements and preparing materials and supplies, you still need to check to make sure that they have been done.
2. ____ In most organizations, Mondays and Fridays are good times on which to hold workshops because there aren't so many meetings on those days.
3. ____ The only really important information that participants need before a workshop is the date, time, and place.
4. ____ You can help participants prepare for training by sending them a brief, relevant pre-work assignment.
5. ____ The room and the way it is set up can play a significant role in the success of a training program.

You will not always be responsible for or involved in everything that needs to be done before a workshop—for example, such tasks as scheduling the workshop, notifying participants, and arranging for a facility might have been done before you come onto the scene. But sometimes you will do or oversee all the preparatory work yourself, and there are some tasks that only you can do. And even if you don't do all the tasks yourself, you need to make sure that they have been done.

Preparing for a workshop typically includes scheduling the training; notifying and preparing participants; reserving a training room and planning the room setup; reserving equipment; preparing materials and supplies; confirming arrangements and make contingency plans; and preparing yourself to conduct training. Checklists, such as the workshop materials checklist shown on page 179, will help you keep track during the process and make sure that you are ready to go on training day.

Preparing for a Workshop

Here's an overview of the tasks involved in preparing for a workshop:

- Schedule the training.
- Select and notify participants.
- Reserve the room and equipment.
- Plan the room setup.
- Prepare or obtain materials and supplies.
- Confirm arrangements and make contingency plans.
- Prepare yourself to conduct training.

Scheduling the Training

THINK ABOUT IT

Have you ever scheduled an event that involved a lot of people—a workshop, a conference, or an important meeting?

- What process did you follow?

_____

_____

_____

_____

- What challenges came up and how did you address them?

_____

_____

_____

_____

Scheduling a workshop can be tricky because there is so much to consider: When will the participants, the facilities, and the necessary equipment all be available? What dates need to be avoided because of other events, deadlines, or other potential conflicts? Without careful scheduling, some participants may not be able to attend or will have their attention elsewhere. You might have to settle for a room that is too small, too large, too noisy, too uncomfortable, or too inconvenient. You might be missing essential equipment because other people are using it.

When you schedule a workshop, you need to consider a number of factors, such as how soon the training needs to be held; when the participants, the facility, and the necessary equipment are available; and how soon the materials can be ready. Let's take a closer look at those questions.

- *Urgency of the training.* Does it matter whether the workshop is held by a certain date, or by the end of the quarter or the fiscal year? Is the training tied to the introduction of a new product launch, new regulations, or a new system? Even if training isn't tied to another event or deadline, how important is it that the learners' performance change quickly?

- *Participants' schedules.* Trainers often make the mistake of setting dates and arranging for the room, only to learn that a significant number of the participants will be attending a conference or working on year-end reports at that time. You can't have a workshop without participants, so before fixing the dates in stone, make sure that they have no conflicting responsibilities and that their managers can release them on those dates. That's not always easy to do, especially when the participants' jobs involve a lot of travel. You might have to "float" several possible dates to find the ones that work for the most people and get help from a manager or administrator who handles people's calendars.

  As a rule, try to avoid scheduling workshops on Mondays, Fridays, weeks with three-day weekends, and the weeks before and after a major holiday. Summer can be a difficult time to schedule training because it's hard to work around people's vacations, although in some industries, summer is the slowest season. Think about the industry: CPAs are usually be swamped during tax season, and retailers during the weeks leading up to the holidays.

- *Facility availability and accessibility.* The training room can play a significant role in the success of a workshop. I've had to deliver training in such inappropriate spaces as lunchrooms where people wandered in and out all day to use the vending machines and cavernous lecture halls with fixed chairs all facing front. In such spaces, it requires considerable effort to establish and maintain an environment that is conducive to learning.

Find out what's available on the dates you're considering. Look for a room that's not too big, and not too small, has good light, has a door that can be closed, and that can be set up with tables and chairs instead of fixed seating. Choose a location that is convenient for as many people as possible, and consider their accessibility needs. You don't want a room that's up a flight of stairs if you are likely to have a participant in a wheelchair. (There's more on room setup later.)

● *Equipment availability.* Do you need an LCD projector for a PowerPoint presentation? Several flip-chart easels for small group discussions? A DVD player and television monitors? Computers? Other equipment? In some organizations, trainers and meeting planners compete for limited supplies of certain kinds of equipment. Find out when the things you need will be available.

● *Time needed to prepare and obtain materials.* As you learned in Chapter 5, developing training materials can take some time. If you'll be using anything that needs to be custom-developed, such as a workbook, videos, or software, find out when those items will be ready before settling on a date. Also find out when any new products, equipment, forms, or procedures that are part of the program will be available.

> ## Consider When Scheduling
> - Urgency of the training
> - Participants' schedules
> - Time of week and time of year
> - Facility availability and accessibility
> - Equipment availability
> - Time needed to prepare and obtain materials
> - Availability of guest speakers

● *Availability of guest speakers.* If guest speakers, such as company executives or subject-matter experts, will be an important part of the program, it's a good idea to check on their availability before scheduling the training. That's especially important if the people you're inviting are likely to have very busy calendars or if they will need to travel.

Training Fundamentals: Pfeiffer Essential Guides to Training Basics.
Copyright © 2010 by John Wiley & Sons, Inc.
Reproduced by permission of Pfeiffer, an Imprint of Wiley. www.Pfeiffer.com

Check What You Know

Which would be the best way for Francesca to notify and prepare the customer service representatives for training?

1. ____ Send out a notification e-mail with the details—brief description of the program, time, and place—along with the customer service manual and a request that participants read it carefully before the workshop.

2. ____ Send a "welcome" e-mail with the details—the time, date, and location; the reason the training is being held; the learning objectives and the agenda; a relevant question to think about; and your contact information.

3. ____ Ask the participants' managers to tell them that they have been signed up for training and tell them when and where it is being held.

In Chapter 2, you learned that adults like to be actively involved in their learning process. That involvement should start before training begins. In fact, the way in which people find out about a training program can affect their ability to learn. The more engaged and interested they are when the program begins, the more likely it is that they will achieve the learning objectives.

The problem is that people are selected for and notified about training in different ways. It's great when participants have actually been involved in the design process—but that's rare. It's also good when they have chosen to sign up because they are eager to learn about the subject. But in many cases, training is mandatory; in others, all or some of the participants have been "strongly encouraged" to attend. In fact, many people learn that they are expected to attend a workshop only when they receive a formal or informal notification from their manager, human resources, or the trainer.

You may not have much control over how people are selected for training or how they learn that they will be expected to participate, but there are steps you can take to stimulate their interest and begin the process of engaging them. The most important of those steps is making sure that they understand what's in it for them—how the training will benefit them. As Bob Pike says:

. . . people are tuned to the radio station WII-FM. What's In It For Me? . . . you cannot motivate other people . . . but you can create a climate or an environment in which a person is self-motivating.

Bob Pike,
Creative Training Techniques

Here are some of the things that you can do to help ensure that participants arrive ready to learn:

- If possible, meet with participants before training begins to discuss the reasons for training, the learning objectives, what will be covered, and the ways in which the training will benefit them.

- If possible, meet with or send an e-mail to participants' managers to make sure they know their employees are signed up for the workshop and help them understand the importance of the training. Include the logistical details so they will know when people will be away from work and where they will be; the reasons the training is being held and how it will benefit them, the participants, and the organization; the learning objectives; and a way to contact you with questions. Suggest ways in which they can support the participants and help them apply what they learn to their jobs.

- Send participants a "welcome" e-mail. Introduce yourself and the training program. Say why the program is being held and how it will benefit them. Include the logistical details, the learning objectives, and the agenda. Provide your contact information and encourage participants to get in touch if they have questions. To help prepare participants for training, you can also include a question or suggested activity that starts people thinking about what they will be learning.

Sample "Welcome" e-Mail

Dear Mark,

As you know, you are scheduled to attend the Meeting Planning for Team Leaders workshop that will be held on Tuesday, April 7, in the Bayside Training Room. We'll have the Continental breakfast ready by 8:45 so you can get settled and meet some of the other participants. The workshop will begin promptly at 9:00.

This workshop will provide practical tools and techniques that you can use immediately to plan and conduct meetings that make the best use of everyone's time and achieve specific goals. You'll learn how to decide whether a meeting is necessary and who needs to be there, prepare a realistic agenda, manage discussions to keep things on track, help the group solve problems and make decisions, and more. For more detail, please see the workshop objectives and agenda attached to this message.

There are two things I need from you:

1. Please complete the attached questionnaire and send it to me by March 31. Your responses will help me make sure that the workshop meets your needs. I will not show them to anyone else.
2. Also complete the attached "Best and Worst Meetings" worksheet and bring it with you to the workshop. You will use the worksheet in one of the opening activities.

If you have questions before we meet on April 7, I'll be glad to answer them by e-mail or phone. My contact information is at the bottom of this message. I look forward to meeting and working with you.

Sincerely,

Sample Pre-Workshop Questionnaire

MEETING PLANNING FOR TEAM LEADERS
PRE-WORKSHOP QUESTIONNAIRE

Please answer the questions below and return the completed questionnaire to me by March 31. I will use the information only for planning purposes and will not share it with anyone else.

Your name and position: _____

How long have you been in this position? _____

Please indicate your reasons for attending this workshop (check all that apply)

❏ Interested in the topic
❏ Think the information will be useful
❏ Encouraged by my manager
❏ Required by my manager
❏ Other (please specify): _____

What skills would you like to improve and what information would you like me to cover during this workshop?

_____

_____

_____

_____

Please list any questions or concerns you have about the workshop:

_____

_____

_____

_____

Thanks for your help!

- Give participants some pre-work. A brief, relevant pre-work assignment can get people thinking about the topic of the program, what they're going to learn, and how the information will be useful to them. You might pose some questions for them to consider, ask them to complete a self-assessment, or assign some reading or research. But keep in mind that people are busy. If you send something for them to read, keep it brief. If you ask them to do some research, make sure it's something they can do quickly and easily. If you want them to complete a questionnaire, limit the number of questions.

When you send out a pre-work assignment, explain how it relates to the training program: Will you be discussing the reading or the research during the workshop? Will participants receive the report that results from an assessment you've asked them to take? Will you be using the responses from their questionnaire to make sure the workshop meets their needs? If it's important that everyone complete the pre-work, ask them to send you something by a specific date and then follow up if you haven't received it.

Sample Pre-Work Assignment

MEETING PLANNING FOR TEAM LEADERS WORKSHOP, APRIL 7, 2009, 8:45–5:00, BAYSIDE TRAINING ROOM

So that we can make the best use of our time during this workshop, please take ten or twenty minutes to think about meetings that you've attended and answer the questions below. Bring the completed worksheet with you to the workshop. You'll use it during one of the opening activities.

1. Please describe a meeting that you attended that you felt was necessary and productive. What was the purpose of the meeting? What are some of the things that the facilitator or meeting leader did that made it a productive use of time?

   _____

   _____

   _____

   _____

   _____

   _____

2. Please describe a meeting that you felt was not a good use of your time. What was the purpose of the meeting? Was the purpose clear? What could the facilitator or meeting leader have done to improve that meeting?

   _____

   _____

   _____

   _____

   _____

   _____

Check What You Know

Which of the room setups shown on the following pages are likely to convey the message that "this is a learner-centered workshop," encourage participants to communicate with one another and the trainer, and facilitate activities? Why?

1. Rectangular conference table
2. Round tables
3. Rectangular tables, classroom style
4. Rectangular tables, chevron shape
5. U-shaped conference table

Rectangular Conference Table

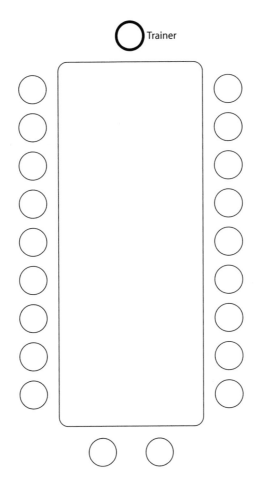

Round Tables

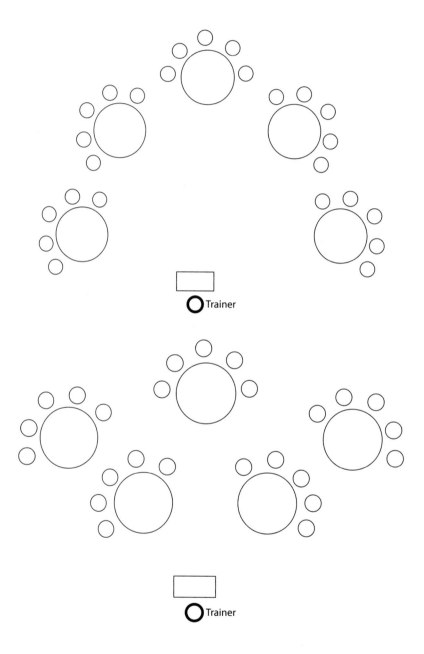

Rectangular Tables, Classroom Style

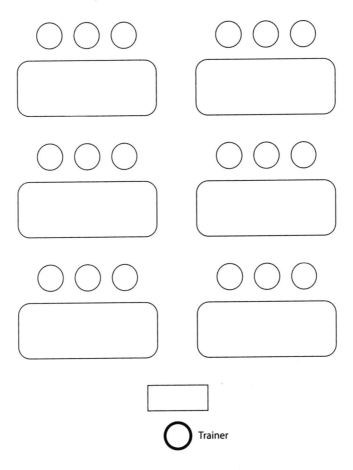

Trainer

Implementing Training Programs

175

Rectangular Tables, Chevron Shape

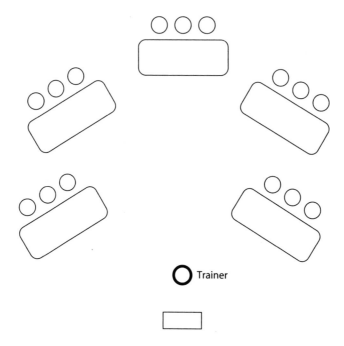

Trainer

U-Shaped Conference Table

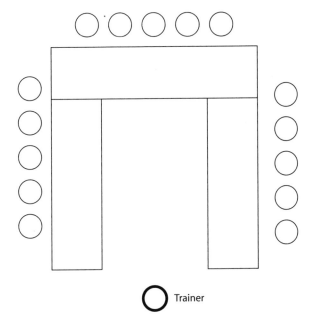

Trainer

Putting on a workshop is a little like putting on a play. You can do a play with only actors on a bare stage—but the set, lighting, special effects, costumes, and props make it a more complete experience for the audience. Similarly, you can deliver a workshop almost anywhere, with only you and the participants. But the right room setup makes it a more complete experience for the learners—and a more satisfying one for you.

It's worth a little effort to find the right room, one that's large enough for participants to work comfortably without crowding, but not so cavernous that people feel overwhelmed by the space. Try your best to avoid rooms that offer only fixed theater-style seating. That setup puts the spotlight on you and makes interaction nearly impossible. Also try to avoid rooms with a single fixed conference table unless the group is very small—six or seven people at most. The people along the sides will have trouble seeing one another, and it will be difficult for people to work on activities in small groups.

Planning the Room Setup

As long as there are no fixed seats or tables, you usually have several options for configuring the room setup. For a workshop during which participants will spend much of their time talking and working with one another, I find that the ideal setup is round tables, with four to six people at a table and enough space between tables so that I can easily walk between them. If round tables are not available, rectangular tables arranged in a chevron shape achieves similar objectives. Whatever setup you use, make sure that participants can easily see you, one another, the flip charts, and the screen (for slides).

Unless you like the idea of moving furniture around on the day of the workshop, don't rely on verbal communications with the people in charge of the room setup. Put your requirements in writing and provide a diagram of the configuration you want.

The Comfort Factor

Have you ever spent hours sitting in an uncomfortable chair, in an overheated or freezing cold room that was badly lit and poorly ventilated? It's difficult—even impossible—to concentrate in those kinds of environments. When considering training rooms, rate them on the comfort factor:

- Comfortable chairs
- Good lighting
- Good ventilation
- Controllable temperature

Reserving the Equipment

As mentioned above, the people running training programs and those running meetings often share a limited supply of projectors, screens, television monitors, flip-chart easels, and other equipment. Even when you hold workshops at off-site venues such as hotels and conference centers, there might not be enough equipment to go around. Make equipment reservations when you reserve the training room—and make them in writing.

Arranging for Refreshments

People will feel more welcome and be more comfortable if refreshments of some kind are available. Providing refreshments has the added benefit of

Sample Workshop Materials Checklist

Today's Date: _____

Workshop Title:_____

Workshop Date and Location: _____

Action	Date Taken	Notes
❑ Participants' welcome letter sent		
❑ Pre-work assignments sent		
❑ Training room configuration to facility manager		
❑ Equipment ordered		
❑ Refreshments ordered		
❑ Participant materials prepared		
❑ Trainer materials prepared		
❑ Activity materials prepared or obtained		
❑ Reminders sent to participants		
❑ Confirmed facility, room setup, equipment, and refreshments		

encouraging people to stay in the room during breaks. If possible, provide coffee, tea, water, juice, and something to eat, such as fruit, sweet rolls, or bagels in the morning, sodas and water, fruit, and something to nibble on in the afternoon. Unless you are bringing in refreshments yourself, place the order when you make the room and equipment reservations.

Preparing or Obtaining Materials and Supplies

You need lots of things to run a workshop, from trainer's guides and participant handouts to marking pens and masking tape. Leave yourself plenty of time to prepare or obtain everything. Try to have everything ready early enough so that you can spend the last few days preparing yourself to conduct the workshop. Leave extra time if materials or supplies need to be shipped to the workshop site. The checklist below can be helpful, or you can use it as a model to create your own.

Confirming Arrangements and Making Contingency Plans

The experienced trainer is a close friend of Murphy and his law of random perversity. A trainer knows that "If something can go wrong, it will."

Elaine Biech,
Training for Dummies

I've arrived on workshop day to find that another trainer is using "my" room, the handouts aren't there, the room is set up for a lecture when the workshop includes lots of discussions and small-group activities, there are only three sheets of paper on the single flip-chart pad, all but one of the marking pens has dried up, even that participants were under the impression that the workshop started an hour later—or, in one instance, on another day.

After a few such experiences, I learned my lesson: avoid problems by checking and double-checking everything and come prepared with contingency plans in case something goes wrong. Some tips:

- Get written confirmation of room and equipment reservations, with the names of people to contact if there are problems. Confirm the reservations a week or so ahead of time and check again the day before the workshop.

Make sure the equipment request includes extra paper for flip-chart easels, cables to connect your laptop to the projector, and any other accessories you may need.

- Discuss the room setup options with the people responsible for providing the room. Tell them exactly what you want and back up your request with written instructions—including a diagram. If the room can be set up the day before the workshop, check the setup yourself. If not, contact those responsible for setup the day before to make sure they understand the instructions and answer any questions.

- Unless you are bringing all the materials and supplies yourself, leave enough time for them to be delivered or shipped to the training site. Then check to make sure that they have arrived.

- Pack a survival kit. Have you ever gone camping and forgotten the bug spray? It's a little item that would have made a big difference to your experience. Little items can also make a big difference to your training. Bring along things you might need, such as good marking pens, painter's tape for putting flip-chart pages up on the wall, extra writing tablets, and a master copy of the participant handouts in print or on a flash drive so you can have them printed quickly if the participant materials fail to arrive.

- Send a friendly reminder to participants a day or two before the workshop. Keep it brief, but include some tidbit of new information or a question for them to think about. Remind them of the time, place, and what they are supposed to bring. Ask them to get in touch with you if they have questions or if something has come up that will keep them from attending. If you've invited a guest speaker or an expert for a demonstration, also send a polite note and/or give the person a call a day or two ahead of time. If you send the reminder by e-mail or leave a phone message, ask the person to respond so that you know the message was received.

- Make back-up plans. Ask yourself, "What if . . . ?" "What if the DVD player doesn't work? I run out of flip-chart paper? The room setup is wrong and can't be changed? There aren't enough participant workbooks (or computers) to go around? The guest speaker doesn't show up? Lunch doesn't arrive?" Try to imagine what might go wrong during each segment of the workshop and decide what you could do if that should happen.

To Avoid or Minimize Problems

- Get written confirmation of room and equipment reservations.
- Know who to contact if there are problems.
- Confirm the reservations a week ahead of time and check again the day before the workshop.
- Make sure people setting up the room know exactly what you want and provide a diagram to avoid misunderstandings.
- If possible, check the setup yourself the day before the workshop.
- Leave enough time for materials and supplies to be delivered or shipped and check to see that they have arrived.
- Pack a survival kit.
- Send friendly reminders to participants and guest speakers.
- Make backup plans, just in case.

Getting Ready to Conduct Training

Check What You Know

Once she's made and double-checked all the arrangements and materials, what are some things that Francesca can do to prepare herself to deliver a great workshop?

_____

_____

_____

_____

People who are good at what they do don't get that way by accident, and they don't rely on chance for success. Top attorneys prepare carefully before arguing a case, even though they may have argued many before. Top tennis players practice before big matches, even though they have already spent hundreds of hours on the court. And successful trainers prepare themselves for every workshop they conduct. No matter what kinds of training they do or how long they've been conducting workshops, they all have the same mantra: Prepare and Practice, Prepare and Practice. That's the best way to increase your confidence, project a self-assured image from the moment the participants walk into the room, and keep the workshop running smoothly so participants will learn from and enjoy the experience. Here's how:

- *Think about the participants.* If you were involved in the process of designing the workshop, you already know a lot about the participants, and you might even know all or some of them personally. You might have had the opportunity to contact them ahead of time and ask for information about their expectations for training. But in some situations, you will not know much more than what jobs they do and their positions in their organization—sometimes you'll be given a roster listing participants' names, and that will be that.

  Even if you know very little about the participants, think about what you do know or can assume. Try to see the workshop from their points of view. Why are they attending? Are they likely to be looking forward to the workshop or to see it as taking away from more important tasks? Are there any current organizational issues, such as a change of management, a reorganization, or rumors of a

> ## Getting Ready to Conduct Training
> - Think about the participants.
> - Find a quiet, private place and walk yourself through the workshop.
> - Rehearse key parts of the presentation.
> - Plan a Q&A.

merger, that are likely to affect their attitudes or be distracting? Thinking about the participants reminds you that the purpose of training is to meet their needs, not your own, and focus on ways to engage them right away.

Training Fundamentals: Pfeiffer Essential Guides to Training Basics.
Copyright © 2010 by John Wiley & Sons, Inc.
Reproduced by permission of Pfeiffer, an Imprint of Wiley. www.Pfeiffer.com

- *Find a quiet, private place and walk yourself through the workshop*—think about what you will do first, second, and so on. Visualize yourself greeting the participants, opening the workshop, introducing the activities, and leading the discussions. If you think it will be helpful, make yourself a "cheat sheet" with important points and reminders.

- *Rehearse key parts of the presentation.* It's great if you can do this in the training room itself, with the slides and other media you will be using. But no matter where you rehearse, do it on your feet. Speak aloud, the way you will deliver the workshop. Practice delivering the opening, introducing the activities, delivering key content, demonstrating, explaining, making transitions. This kind of rehearsal is especially important the first time you deliver a specific workshop, and even more so when the workshop was designed by someone else.

- *Plan a Q&A.* Think about the questions that participants are likely to ask and decide how you will answer them. If any of the answers involve statistics, complicated processes, or other information that is difficult to remember, write them down and/or put them on slides. Decide whether to bring reference materials, such as manuals, that you might need in order to respond to questions.

2. Getting Started

Most people want to learn, most people want to cooperate, most people want to be involved, but sometimes they just don't know how.

Bob Pike,
Creative Training Techniques

THINK ABOUT IT

Here are descriptions of the first few minutes of two workshops. In which workshop would you be most likely to feel welcome, interested, and ready to learn? Why?

1. ___ When you come into the room at 8:50, the trainer, Jane, greets you at the door. She helps you find a seat, gives you a workbook, tells you to help yourself to beverages and fruit, and suggests that you read the information on the opening page of the workbook while you wait for the workshop to begin. At 9:00, Jane opens the workshop. She introduces herself, gives a brief description of the purpose of the workshop, and asks you to introduce yourself to someone you do not know. Then she gives you a few minutes to talk with the people at your table about your expectations for the workshop and how you think what you learn will be useful to you.

2. ___ When you come into the room at 8:50, the trainer, Cedric, is fiddling with the cables that connect his laptop to the projector—something doesn't seem to be working right. You look around for coffee and find it in a far corner of the room on a table with a partly open box filled with workbooks, note pads, and other supplies. You take a seat at one of the tables and say hi to some of the other participants. Two people at your table are flipping through the pages of a workbook, so you help yourself to one of the workbooks in the box and sit down again. It is now 9:05. Cedric turns on the projector. A slide with the workshop title and the word "Welcome!" appears on the screen. Cedric counts the people in the room, and says, "We're still waiting for a few people. We'll start in a minute." He sits down at the table and pages through a binder. Two more people arrive. Finally, about 9:15, Cedric stands up and says, "Let's get started," and flashes the workshop objectives on the screen.

Experienced runners know that missing the start can mean losing the race. Experienced trainers know that the way a workshop begins can affect the entire training session, and when they lose people at the start, it can be hard to get them back.

A trainer like Cedric who appears disorganized and uninterested, and who does not capture participants' interest at the beginning of the workshop, may have difficulty establishing an environment that is conducive to learning. Jane, on the other hand, did several things to make sure that people would be ready to learn: She arrived early enough to make sure everything was ready by the time the participants arrived; greeted people and made them feel welcome; gave participants who arrived early something to do; got started on time even though not everyone was there; and began with activities that got people talking to one another and thinking about why they were there.

Jane opened her workshop in a way that sets it up for success by following these guidelines:

- *Arrive early.* Make it a rule to arrive at least an hour before a workshop is scheduled to begin—earlier if the workshop requires an unusual amount of setup time. There's always something that needs to be done: check sight lines and adjust the room setup; make sure you have enough flip-chart paper; hook up your laptop to the projector and test the connections; post prepared flip-chart pages; put out workbooks and name tents; arrange your script and other materials so they will be at hand when you need them; make sure refreshments arrive and are set up in the right place; and do other tasks so that everything is ready when participants arrive. This early arrival also gives you time to make yourself comfortable in the workshop space. I've found that taking a few minutes to walk around the room, visualize the participants in their seats, and practice my opening remarks helps me relax and feel confident that I can deliver a great workshop.

- *Greet people when they arrive.* Nothing makes people feel more unwelcome than not being noticed when they walk into a room. Finish your preparations early enough so that you can focus on the participants as they arrive. Greet them with a smile and introduce yourself. Show them where the refreshments are and where they can sit. Think about having something for early arrivers to do while they wait: something to read, a question to think about, a short quiz to answer—something that gets them thinking about the workshop instead of the e-mail piling up in their inboxes.

Start on Time

Check What You Know

1. What are some reasons that it is important to start a workshop on time?

   _____

   _____

   _____

   _____

2. What are some strategies for getting started on time?

   _____

   _____

   _____

   _____

When the American Conservatory Theatre moved from Chicago to San Francisco in the early 1970s, they instituted a policy of starting their productions on time—they actually made latecomers wait in the lobby until a scene break. That policy came as quite a shock to San Francisco theatergoers, who routinely arrived late, their experience having been that the curtain never went up until ten or even twenty minutes past curtain time.

When scheduled events routinely start late, people routinely show up late. It's a vicious cycle: late start leads to late arrivals which leads to late start . . . you get the idea. To demonstrate respect for the people who do come on time and make it easier to stick to your timetable, establish a policy of starting on time, even if not everyone is there.

Of course, that's easier said than done. Here are some strategies that I and other trainers have used:

> Announce: "Coffee and bagels at 8:45; workshop begins at 9:00 sharp."

> Make sure that something important happens right at the start of every workshop so people quickly learn that they will miss something if they are late.

> Send out a text or instant message reminder half an hour before the workshop begins.

> Enlist the help of participants' managers—make sure they support the training and convey an expectation that people will be there on time.

● *Engage participants right away.* Trainers often begin workshops with a long-winded description of the purpose of the workshop, the learning objectives, and the agenda, sometimes preceded or followed by going around the room and asking participants to introduce themselves to the group. That's a very trainer-centered way to start a workshop. Instead, set a positive tone and establish a climate conducive to learning by doing a brief activity that gets people talking to one another and participating actively right away. The better able you are to get the workshop off the ground in a way that engages participants and gets them involved, the more successful your workshop will be.

● *Help participants see what's in it for them.* Keep in mind that adult learners need to see the relevance of what they are learning and recognize how it will benefit them. Take a few minutes at the beginning of the workshop to help participants see how what they are going to learn will make a difference for them.

● *Tell participants what to expect.* Before launching into the first segment of the workshop, give participants the "big picture." Elicit participants' own objectives—what they want to accomplish during the workshop.

Then explain the learning objectives and the agenda, showing them how the objectives and agenda items relate to what they want to accomplish.

- *Convey enthusiasm, confidence, and a positive tone.* Passive, lethargic, disinterested trainers quickly find that their participants are . . . you guessed it: passive, lethargic, and disinterested. It's not necessary to leap around and perform tricks, but your enthusiasm, confidence, and positive attitude need to show. If you want learners to believe that what they are learning is worthwhile, you have to believe it yourself.

- *Give people a chance to ask questions and voice concerns.* Before moving on, make sure that people understand the agenda and give them a chance to ask any questions they may have about the workshop content and structure. Also give them a chance to express any concerns they may have about the training. Do this quickly. Don't feel that you need to address everything in the moment—write any unanswered questions and concerns on a flip-chart page, post the page, and promise that you'll get to them during the workshop (and keep that promise!).

What's an Icebreaker?

"Icebreaker" is a catch-all term for an activity that is used within the first few minutes of a workshop. Icebreakers are sometimes considered time-wasters, frivolous activities that have no real purpose and add nothing to the learning experience. But the best icebreakers serve an important purpose: they help people get to know one another and feel comfortable in the training environment, stimulate interest in the subject, and encourage active participation right from the beginning.

Tips for Getting Started

- Arrive early so you are ready when participants arrive.
- Greet people when they come into the room.
- Start on time.
- Engage participants right away.
- Help participants see what's in it for them.
- Tell participants what to expect.
- Convey enthusiasm, confidence, and a positive tone.
- Give people a chance to ask questions and voice concerns.

THINK ABOUT IT

Think about a time when felt nervous when you were standing in front of a group during a meeting or to make a presentation.

1. How did the nervous feeling manifest themselves?
    What symptoms did you experience?

    _____

    _____

    _____

2. What did you do to handle the symptoms of nervousness?

    _____

    _____

    _____

3. What could you do to reduce the symptoms of nervousness during a workshop?

    _____

    _____

    _____

Handling Nervousness

All trainers feel nervous at one time or another, just as all performers feel stage fright. Experience reduces the symptoms, but even experienced trainers sometimes find themselves nervous the first time they deliver a new workshop or work with a new group of learners.

Here are some suggestions for reducing nervousness and anxiety and for handling the symptoms when they do come up:

- *Prepare and practice.* Nervousness often results from a lack of confidence. The better prepared you are and the more you have practiced your delivery, the less likely it will be that you will experience a high degree of nervousness and anxiety. In high-stakes situations, where it is especially important that the workshop go well, put extra time into planning and practice.

- *Recognize when you need to learn more about the subject.* You don't need to be an expert in the subject matter to deliver a great workshop. But you do need to know enough so that you appear credible. Talk through the workshop with someone who is an expert and can reassure you that your level of knowledge is fine or help fill in the missing pieces.

- *Make backup plans.* No matter how carefully you prepare, last-minute problems such as room mix-ups or missing or malfunctioning equipment often crop up, triggering a wave of anxiety. Thinking ahead of time about what problems might come up and what you can do to handle them keeps you focused and confident so that you can present a calm, relaxed image to the learners.

- *Be at your best.* Delivering a workshop can be stressful. To reduce stress, you need to eat well, get enough sleep and exercise, and take time for activities that help you relax.

- *Get comfortable in the training room.* Walk around the room. Use the equipment. Check the sight lines. Sit at a table so you can look at the room through a participant's eyes. Stand in front of the room and practice the opening.

- *Make eye contact with participants.* Trainers often experience a rush of nervous systems at the beginning of a workshop. Eye contact establishes a human connection that can reduce that nervousness. Make eye contact with people when you greet them. Make eye contact with a few people in the group before you launch into your opening. Then continue to make eye contact with individuals in the audience as you speak and as you listen while they are speaking.

- *Move.* Trainers who hold themselves rigidly, with their knees locked and their feet fixed firmly to the floor, often find it difficult to relax. Move around as you speak and listen to participants. Take a few steps toward the group, or move from side to side. Don't wander or pace, just move naturally.

- *Slow down.* When people are nervous, they often speed up their speech, as if to get it over with as quickly as possible. When that happens, force yourself to slow down. Pause to collect your thoughts, let participants think about how to respond to a question, and give participants a chance to process what they hear.

- *If necessary, acknowledge your nervousness.* This suggestion is controversial. Many trainers believe that it is not a good idea to tell an audience that you are feeling nervous. My own feeling is that when the symptoms are obvious—your voice is shaking, you're dropping papers and props on the floor, or you're tripping over equipment cords—learners can become uncomfortable. It can help to take a deep breath, make eye contact with a few people in the audience, and acknowledge what you are feeling: "I'm sorry, but I seem to be feeling a little nervous today." Take another deep breath, smile, and then, when you feel ready, continue.

3. Running the Workshop

Check What You Know

What are some things that you can do to keep a workshop running smoothly and on track?

_____

_____

_____

_____

_____

_____

Running a workshop is a little like juggling: You have to keep several balls in the air at one time. People who are new to training are often surprised by how difficult it can be to follow the script while showing slides, writing on flip-chart pages, fielding questions, giving instructions, facilitating discussions, and managing group and individual behavior. "I'm exhausted after every workshop," one new trainer told me. "I feel as if I have to keep pouring energy into the group."

I remember feeling that way. But after I'd been training for a while, I started to feel energized after a workshop, instead of enervated. I've found that other experienced trainers felt the same. "I love training," a colleague who runs several workshops a month told me. "It feels great when people tell me how much they've learned and how much they've enjoyed the day. I love their questions, and that little light that comes on when they try something new and it works!"

But it's natural to find it hard to relax and enjoy what you're doing when you start something new. A novice tennis player is trying to remember and control so many things that it's hard to simply enjoy the game. It's the same with a novice trainer—there are so many things to do and control that it's hard to settle back and find pleasure in the experience. Don't worry if that's how it is with you at first—things will change after you have been training for a while. In the meantime, there are some things you can do to keep everything running smoothly, stay on track, and increase the chances that both you and the learners will have a positive experience.

- *Pay attention.* Tune into the group from the moment that people walk in the door, and stay tuned in for the entire workshop. Pay attention to what participants say and do, to their nonverbal behavior, their tones of voice. You can quickly tell from their body language, tone, and facial expressions whether they are engaged and interested, or whether they are confused, bored, or upset. You'll also learn who likes to speak up, who prefers to learn by listening, and who presents behavior problems that may need to be addressed before they interfere with the workshop.

THINK ABOUT IT

Imagine that while you are speaking to the group, one participant is sitting up straight in his chair with his eyes on you, while another is slumped in her seat with her arms crossed. Both of those participants are sending nonverbal messages. What do you think those messages might be?

_____

_____

_____

_____

_____

_____

The first participant appears to be interested and attentive. The second appears to be bored, and possibly even upset. The more attention you pay to the participants, the more quickly you can pick up those kinds of nonverbal signals and respond in the appropriate way.

- *Be flexible.* For me, one of the most fascinating things about being a trainer is that every group is so different. Some activities work perfectly with some groups and bomb with others. Some groups get new concepts easily, while others need lots more explanation. As a trainer, you always need to be ready to shift gears and to remain flexible enough to go off script when necessary. For example, I always come prepared with optional activities and content so I can make substitutions. And when something completely unexpected comes up, I try to be ready to stop or significantly change the workshop to respond to the group's needs.

- *Stay on track.* Suppose you have two days to drive halfway across the country to attend a family reunion. There are lots of tempting side trips along the way: you've always wanted to visit that national monument, and you read about a beautiful lake just a few miles off the freeway. But you might not be able to make those side trips because they would take more time than you have and make it difficult to get to the reunion on time.

    Side trips in a workshop—discussions that go off track, questions that take you into interesting territory but are not directly related to the topic—also use up time and make it difficult to reach the destination. One of your key roles as a trainer is to keep the workshop on track so that participants can achieve the learning objectives. That means keeping an eye on the time, bringing discussions to a close when they've served their purpose, and stopping activities when the time runs out so you can move on.

- *Handle problems right away.* Little problems can quickly balloon into big problems that can ruin a workshop. There will always be something you haven't considered: last-minute room changes, malfunctioning equipment, noise, fire drills, crises that take people out of the workshop, disruptive participants . . . the list goes on.

    Problems fall into several categories: Those you can control, and those you can't; those the group is aware of and those only you know about; and those that are serious enough to interfere with the workshop and those that are just annoying. If the problem is beyond your control, such as a last-minute room change into a room that's too small, you need to make the best of the situation and

> ## Tips for Staying on Track
> - Start the workshop on time, even if not everyone is there.
> - Establish the expectation that people will return on time from breaks.
> - Keep your eye on the clock and on the agenda.
> - Manage discussions to keep them on the topic.
> - Use a "parking lot"—a flip-chart page for side issues so you can capture them and move on.
> - Stop activities when the time is up or the objective has been achieved.

move on. If participants are aware of the problem, you might also need to acknowledge it, even if you can't change the situation.

But it's important to do whatever you can to deal with real, ongoing problems that interfere with the group's ability to learn. If the room temperature is so hot or so cold that people can't concentrate, find someone who can adjust the temperature or switch you into a different room. If half the participants are called out to deal with an emergency, see whether the group would be able to reschedule the workshop.

With experience, you'll learn to tell the difference between problems that need to be—or can be—handled and those that can be lived with. Sometimes, in fact, an apparent problem isn't much of a problem after all. I've become very upset at a last-minute change of room, only to find (when I calmed down) that the new room was perfectly fine. I've rolled my eyes when the sound from a DVD playing in the next room drifted through the walls, but simply acknowledged the noise and raised my voice a little until the DVD was over, waiting until the break to speak to the other trainer. When a fire drill forced us into the parking lot for fifteen minutes, I easily obtained the group's agreement to recoup the missing time by doing part of an activity over lunch.

> ## Tips for Handling Disruptive Behavior
>
> - Establish ground rules regarding behavior that can be invoked if necessary.
> - Don't let disruptive behavior continue.
> - Focus on the behavior, not the person.
> - Treat people politely and with respect.
> - Avoid arguments.
> - Do not take challenges personally.
> - If necessary, speak to disruptive participants privately.
> - If disruptive behavior continues, ask the person to leave.

- *Handle disruptive or offensive behavior right away.* Participants who start side conversations, continually challenge what you and others say, demand center stage, make snide or offensive comments, openly refuse to participate in activities, or engage in other disruptive or offensive behavior poison the learning environment. It's very important to recognize and deal with such behavior right away. You might be able to anticipate it by helping the group establish ground rules that govern behavior, such as "listen while other people are talking," "respect other people's points of view," "no personal attacks," and "give others a chance to speak." But if a participant's disruptive or offensive behavior continues after you've invoked the ground rules, you have to take action. That might mean speaking to the person privately during a break or while others are working on an activity. If behavior still continues, or if it is very disruptive, ask the person to leave.

Quick Quiz

List the three to five key learning points from this chapter that will be most helpful to you.

_____

_____

_____

_____

_____

What's Next?

Starting out in a new field involves learning all the terminology that people use, much of which is unfamiliar, and some of which are ordinary words used in unique ways. You've already encountered some of the language that training professionals commonly use when talking and writing about training. In Chapter 7, you'll find definitions of those terms and others that you are likely to encounter.

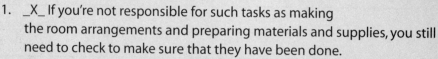

Apply What You Learn

Answer the questions on the worksheet at the end of this chapter to think about how to plan and prepare for your training program and to help it run smoothly.

Answers to Exercises

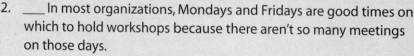

Check What You Know

Which of the following statements do you think are valid?

1. _X_ If you're not responsible for such tasks as making the room arrangements and preparing materials and supplies, you still need to check to make sure that they have been done.
2. ___ In most organizations, Mondays and Fridays are good times on which to hold workshops because there aren't so many meetings on those days.
3. ___ The only really important information that participants need before a workshop is the date, time, and place.
4. _X_ You can help participants prepare for training by sending them a brief, relevant pre-work assignment.
5. _X_ The room and the way it is set up can play a significant role in the success of a training program.

Check What You Know

Which would be the best way for Francesca to notify and prepare the customer service representatives for training?

1. ___ Send out a notification e-mail with the details—brief description of the program, time, and place—along with the customer service manual and a request that participants read it carefully before the workshop.
2. _X_ Send a "welcome" e-mail with the details—the time, date, and location; the reason the training is being held; the learning objectives and the agenda; a relevant question to think about; and your contact information.
3. ___ Ask the participants' managers to tell them that they have been signed up for training and tell them when and where it is being held.

Check What You Know

Which of the room setups shown are most likely to convey the message that "this is a learner-centered workshop," encourage participants to communicate with one another and the trainer, and facilitate activities? Why?

1. Rectangular conference table
2. Round tables
3. Rectangular tables, classroom style
4. Rectangular tables, chevron shape
5. U-shaped conference table

Room setups 2 and 4 encourage participation and communication by making it easy for participants to work together and see one another as well as the trainer.

Planning and Preparing for a Workshop

1. What do you need to keep in mind when scheduling the workshop? Can you choose the dates now? What do you need to know and do before choosing dates?

   _____

   _____

   _____

   _____

2. How will you notify and prepare the participants? Their managers?

   _____

   _____

   _____

   _____

3. What materials and equipment will you need?

   _____

   _____

   _____

   _____

   _____

   _____

   _____

4. What will you do to prepare yourself to conduct training?

_____

_____

_____

_____

_____

_____

5. What problems might come up, and how will you handle them?

_____

_____

_____

_____

_____

_____

_____

_____

_____

_____

_____

_____

_____

_____

_____

7

The Language of Training

Check What You Know

Andy was looking forward to his new job as a training associate, a promotion from the supervisory position he'd held for several years. But he came away from his first day with his head spinning. His new manager, giving him an overview of what the training department did and what his responsibilities would be, used words he'd never heard before: "needs assessment," "icebreaker," "WBT," "behavioral objectives," "front-end analysis," "experiential learning," and "smee," to name a few. Andy didn't feel comfortable asking what those terms meant because he wanted to make a good impression on his first day. But he could see that to communicate with the other trainers, he'd have to get up to speed quickly on the new terminology.

How much do you know about the language of training? Which of the terms that Andy's manager used can you define?

Needs assessment

_____

_____

(Continued)

Icebreaker

_____

_____

WBT

_____

_____

Behavioral objectives

_____

_____

Front-end analysis

_____

_____

Experiential learning

_____

_____

Smee

_____

_____

My first job in training was for a company that developed instructional programs for the U.S. Army. I spent the first three months or so learning the Army's language—the terms and acronyms in the voluminous manuals and documents we needed to scour for content information. (I've managed to forget nearly all of it in the intervening years because I never needed it again.) But I also had to learn another language: the language of training. It took me a while to find out that "OD" meant "organization development," which referred to the things that an organization did to become more effective, efficient, and competitive. That "SME" (pronounced S-M-E or "smee") meant "subject-matter expert," referring to the people who knew how to do something we needed to teach. I don't remember actually learning all those acronyms and terms, but I realized that I understood them one day when a brand-new employee asked me what they meant.

Here's what we'll cover in this chapter:

- Reasons for learning the terminology used in the field of training
- Glossary of training terminology

1. Why Learn the Language of Training?

When you travel in another country, a little understanding of the language makes it easier to get around. If you live there for any length of time, you'll need enough vocabulary to rent an apartment and buy groceries. And if you want to be able to hold conversations about anything beyond the price of vegetables, you'll need to study the language until you can speak and understand it with some degree of fluency.

Every industry and field has its own language. If you know that language, you can grasp certain concepts quickly and clearly when people use it; if you don't know it, they might as well speak Martian—that's how well you'll understand what they say. Learning the special terminology used in an industry or profession is part of learning to do the job. Most people learn it by osmosis because, like Andy, they do not want to appear foolish by asking.

You need some understanding of the language of training when you communicate with other training professionals. You'll need more when you read about training—even some common terms and acronyms might not appear in a dictionary. And if you want to make training your profession, the ability to understand and use training terminology will help you build credibility in the training community.

You've already learned a lot of terminology in the previous chapters of this book. The glossary in this chapter is intended as an introduction to many of the most commonly used and useful terms; just as you eventually pick up essential words of a foreign language by listening to people talk, watching television, and reading signs and newspaper headlines, you'll eventually pick up the language of training as you work in the field.

2. Glossary of Training Terminology

Accelerated learning. An approach to designing training that is based on research into the way the human brain works. Accelerated learning programs use physical activity, creativity, music, images, color, and other methods to help people go beyond what they think they can do, involve them actively in the learning process, and help them learn more quickly.

Action learning. Developed by British Professor Reginald Revans in the 1940s and based on the work of John Dewey, action learning is a process for helping people learn by doing. Learners with differing levels of skills and experience collaborate to analyze a real problem, develop and implement an action plan, implement the plan, draw learning points from the experience, and apply what they learn to future problems.

Andragogy. An approach to learning that is focused on the learners, not on the teacher. The term was coined by a German educator, Alexander Kapp, nearly two centuries ago, but it is now commonly associated with Dr. Malcolm Knowles, a central figure in the field of adult education. See Pedagogy.

Andragogical learning model: A learner-centered approach to learning in which the learners are active and the teacher is a guide whose responsibility is to facilitate the learning process. See Pedagogical Learning Model.

Asynchronous learning. A method of delivering instruction in which there is no real-time interaction—and sometimes, no interaction at all—between the learners and between the learners and the trainer. See Synchronous Learning.

Audience. The learners for whom a training program is designed. See Target Audience.

Auditory learners. According to some theories about the ways in which people learn, auditory learners learn best by hearing information and may remember information more accurately when it has been explained to them.

Authoring tool. Software that is used to produce e-learning programs and media-based learning content.

Avatar. A computer-generated image that represents a person. Learners and trainers can use avatars to interact with one another in virtual training rooms or in simulations.

Baseline. Data about learners' knowledge, skills, and attitudes before training that is used to measure the degree to which training has achieved results.

Behavioral objectives. A description of what learners will be able to do as a result of training. Also called performance objectives, learning objectives, or terminal objectives.

Blended learning. A training program that combines a variety of delivery methods and media to meet organizational goals and the learners' needs.

Bloom's Taxonomy. A classification of levels of intellectual behavior important in learning developed in 1956 by educational psychologist Benjamin Bloom and a group of colleagues. Bloom's taxonomy, which provides a process-oriented method for understanding a learning or training process, identified three overlapping domains of learning: cognitive, psychomotor, and affective, known more commonly as knowledge, skills, and attitude (KSA).

Breakout room. An extra room or space where participants in a workshop can go to work on an activity.

Case study. A detailed description of a real or realistic situation, such as a management or technical problem, that is used to help people learn individually or in groups.

Chunking. The process of breaking information down into easily digestible pieces in order to promote understanding. According to research by psychologist George A. Miller and others, there is a limit on how much information people can grasp and retain at one time, so they learn and remember information better when it is presented in manageable "chunks."

Cognitive skills. Thinking, understanding, reasoning, problem solving, and other mental skills that are used to acquire knowledge.

Collaborative learning. A learning environment or activity in which people learn from one another and work together to solve problems or accomplish a project with little or no assistance from a trainer.

Competency. A knowledge, skill, ability, attitude, or trait that is needed to succeed at a particular task or job.

Competency model. A description of the critical knowledge, skills, abilities, and traits needed to succeed in a specific endeavor, such as a specific job or position. Competency models include competencies that are innate or difficult to learn, as well as those that can be developed or learned.

Computer-based training (CBT). Most commonly refers to training that is delivered via a computer. Also called computer-assisted instruction (CAI), online training, and technology-based training (TBT).

Content. What is being learned—the facts, concepts, processes, procedures, skills, rules, guidelines, techniques, and best practices that people need to learn so they can achieve the objectives of a training program.

Core competencies. See Competency Model.

Courseware. The materials and media that contains the instructional content of a training program.

Criterion-referenced instruction. A comprehensive set of methods developed by Robert Mager that guide the design and delivery of training programs. The program is designed to help learners achieve specific behavioral objectives that are tied to the desired outcome.

Cross-training. The process of preparing team members to be able to carry out one another's tasks and responsibilities. Cross-training provides organizations with flexibility in managing the workforce while helping employees develop new skills.

Deductive learning. Learners begin with generalizations, such as principles, and proceed to specifics, such as examples of how principles are applied. See Inductive Learning.

Delivery method. The method by which training is delivered to the learner, for example: live, in-person workshops; virtual workshops; self-directed e-learning; and self-study print programs.

Demographics. The characteristics used to describe learners, such as age, gender, industry, position, and level of experience; also, specific information about the audience for training, such as group size and location.

Design. The plan for a training program, usually a written document that specifies the learning objectives and delivery method(s) along with an outline of the content, activities, and structure. The design acts as a blueprint to guide the program development. Also called design specifications, training program design, or design document.

Discovery learning. Learning methods in which people draw on their own experience and knowledge to discover facts and relationships for themselves. Developed by psychologist Jerome Bruner, who based his work on that of earlier researchers into the learning process, including Jean Piaget and John Dewey.

Distance learning. Training programs such as e-learning or virtual workshops that are delivered to people who are not all present in the same place at the same time.

e-Learning. Refers to the broad category of training programs that are delivered by computer and on mobile electronic devices.

Enabling objective. An objective that a learner must achieve in order to achieve a learning objective.

Experiential learning. A learning method in which people do something, then analyze and reflect on the experience, identify the key learning points, and think about how to use what they have learned (or apply the learning).

Facilitator's guide. A manual that typically includes an agenda, an outline or script, and other information that a trainer needs to conduct a workshop. Also called an instructor's guide or a trainer guide.

Front-end analysis. See Needs Assessment.

Inductive learning. Learners begin with specifics, such as examples of specific situations, and proceed to generalizations, such as principles or strategies. See Deductive Learning.

Ground rules. Guidelines for behavior during a workshop, such as, "Cell phones off," "Everything we say in this room stays in this room," "Only one person speaks at a time," and "Come back on time from breaks." Ground rules are usually established by the group and the trainer during the opening of the workshop.

Group norms. Similar to ground rules. May include expectations for behavior such as, "Participate actively," "Take risks," and "Ask questions."

Human performance improvement (HPI). The systematic process of discovering and analyzing performance gaps, planning for improvements in performance, designing and developing programs to close performance gaps, implementing the interventions, and evaluating the results.

Icebreaker. An opening activity for a workshop that is designed to help participants get to know one another, feel comfortable participating actively, and, perhaps, to begin thinking about the topic.

Instructional design. The process of analyzing learning needs and designing and developing programs to meet specific needs. See Instructional Systems Design (ISD).

Instructional systems design (ISD). A systematic approach to the process of designing and developing a training program originally developed by the U.S. Department of Defense, later popularized by Dick and Carey (see ADDIE in acronyms, below)

Instructional technology. See Instructional Design. Refers specifically to applying theories and learning models to the instructional design process.

Instructor. A teacher or trainer.

Intranet. A private network that uses technology to share information within an organization.

Job aid. A set of printed or online instructions that a person can follow to do a task.

Job analysis. See Task Analysis.

Kinesthetic learners. According to some theories about the ways in which people learn, kinesthetic learners are "hands-on" learners who can concentrate better and learn more easily when physical movement is involved.

Learning management system (LMS). Software that organizations use to manage their training programs, provide learners with access to content, track data, and more.

Learning objectives. The desired results of training; statements of what learners will be able to do as a result of training. Also referred to as performance objectives, behavioral objectives, and terminal objectives.

Multiple intelligences. A learning model developed by Harvard Professor of Education Howard Gardner, who postulated that we have eight different "intelligences" or skills that we use to solve different kinds of problems.

Needs assessment. The initial systematic investigation that is conducted to identify the gap between desired and actual performance and determine whether training is the best way to close the gap. Also called needs analysis or front-end analysis.

Off-the-shelf learning programs. Training programs that have already been developed and that can be purchased to be used as is or customized to meet specific needs.

Pedagogy. The art, science, or profession of teaching. See Andragogy.

Pedagogical learning model. Describes the traditional teacher-centered approach whereby the teacher is the content expert who imparts knowledge to passive learners. See Andragogical Learning Model.

Peer learning. See Collaborative Learning.

Personal learning environments. Refers to systems that enable learners to control and manage their own learning.

Pilot. A test of a training program with a group that is representative of the target audience in order to discover what's working and what needs to be changed before launching the program. See Validation.

Podcast. Essentially, an audio or video file that is distributed over the Internet and that can be played back on computers and mobile devices. The term podcasting is a blend of the words iPod and broadcasting.

Pre-work. Assignments given to learners in advance of a training program.

Rapid e-learning. Strategies, tools, and processes for developing and delivering e-learning programs more quickly and at a lower cost without sacrificing the ability of the program to achieve results.

Role play. An activity in which learners act out a scenario to try out strategies and practice what they are learning.

Training Fundamentals: Pfeiffer Essential Guides to Training Basics.
Copyright © 2010 by John Wiley & Sons, Inc.
Reproduced by permission of Pfeiffer, an Imprint of Wiley. www.Pfeiffer.com

Return on investment (ROI). A metric that attempts to determine what the organization receives in return for its expenditures on a training program.

Scaffolding. A teaching strategy which builds on learners' prior knowledge and provides support that encourages success as they move to increasingly challenging levels.

Self-directed learning. A training program in which learners themselves determine what, where, and when they will learn and manage their own learning process, often with the help of someone else, such as a human resources or training professional or a manager. See Self-Paced Learning.

Self-paced learning. An asynchronous learning program that people can take on their own, at times and locations of their own choosing, with or without guidance from a trainer or an administrator. See Self-Directed Learning.

Simulation. In training, refers to a live or computer-generated situation or scenario that closely replicates the real world so that people can learn and practice in a realistic but safe situation.

Smile sheets. Colloquial term commonly used to describe the questionnaires used to evaluate participants' initial responses to training.

Social media. Online technologies and practices that people use to share content, opinions, insights, experiences, and perspectives.

Subject-matter expert (SME). Someone who has expert knowledge about a topic, a process, a procedure, or how a job is done.

Synchronous learning. Training programs in which all the learners are learning together at the same time, although not necessarily in the same place. See Asynchronous Learning.

Target audience. The learners—the people for whom a program is intended. Often referred to as "audience."

Task analysis. The process of breaking down a task, job, or responsibility into its component parts and identifying the actions needed to complete it properly. Also called job analysis.

Terminal objectives. See Behavioral Objectives and Learning Objectives.

Trainer. Often used as a synonym for instructor, but can refer to anyone who is involved in the field of training.

Trainer's guide. See Facilitator's Guide.

Training consultant. Usually refers to a training professional who works on a freelance or project basis to provide training services to an organization. Internal trainers are sometimes referred to as consultants, meaning that they serve as consultants to their internal clients.

Training Fundamentals: Pfeiffer Essential Guides to Training Basics.
Copyright © 2010 by John Wiley & Sons, Inc.
Reproduced by permission of Pfeiffer, an Imprint of Wiley. www.Pfeiffer.com

Validation. The process of testing a training program on a representative sample of the target audience to make sure that it works as designed and identify changes that might need to be made before the program is delivered to the learners. See Pilot.

Visual learners. According to some theories about the ways in which people learn, visual learners learn best by seeing information; they prefer using

Alphabet Soup

Every field and industry has its own set of acronyms. They are a useful shorthand method of communication—as long as everyone involved in the communication knows what the letters stand for. Here are a few of the acronyms commonly used in the training field.

ADDIE (Analyze, Design, Develop, Implement, Evaluate—the process of instructional design)
CBT (computer-based training)
CRT (criterion referenced instruction)
ELA (experiential learning activity)
HPI (human performance improvement)
HR (human resources)
HRD (human resource development)
ISD (instructional systems design)
KSA (knowledge, skills, and attitude)
LMS (learning management system)
OD (organization development)
PBT (performance-based instruction)
ROI (return on investment)
SMART (referring to learning objectives, typically: specific, measurable, achievable, relevant, timely)
SME (subject-matter expert)
VoIP (voice-over Internet protocol)
WBT (web-based training)
WIIFM (what's in it for me)

images, pictures, colors, and maps to organize information and communicate with others.

Vodcast. A video podcast.

Voiceover internet protocol (VoIP). The technologies for delivering voice communication over the Internet.

Web-based training (WBT). Training delivered over the Internet or a company's intranet.

Webinar. A live or recorded workshop or seminar that is delivered on a website.

Wiki. A user-edited website on which people can share information.

Workforce learning professional. Another name for a training professional.

What's Next?

In the last chapter of this book, you'll learn about ways in which you can develop your skills as a training professional and make a professional development plan that will start you on your way.

Apply What You Learn

Are there terms you've read or heard that you aren't sure you understand but that don't appear on the list in this chapter? Write them below. Then do a web search to find the definitions (and don't be surprised if you find more than one definition for the same term!).

_____

_____

_____

_____

_____

_____

Training Fundamentals: Pfeiffer Essential Guides to Training Basics.
Copyright © 2010 by John Wiley & Sons, Inc.
Reproduced by permission of Pfeiffer, an Imprint of Wiley. www.Pfeiffer.com

8

On Becoming a Training Professional

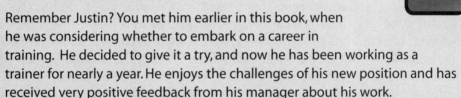

Check What You Know

Remember Justin? You met him earlier in this book, when he was considering whether to embark on a career in training. He decided to give it a try, and now he has been working as a trainer for nearly a year. He enjoys the challenges of his new position and has received very positive feedback from his manager about his work.

"If you think you'd like to stay in this field," Justin's manager says during his annual performance evaluation meeting, "I could give you some suggestions about developing yourself as a training professional."

"That'd be great," Justin replies. "I think that training might be the right career for me, and I've learned a lot this past year. But I know that I've only scratched the surface. There's so much more I need to know about the various kinds of training programs, the theories, the methodology—and what I can do to further my career. I'd really appreciate any help you could give me."

(Continued)

If you were Justin's manager, what would you suggest that he do to learn more about the field of training and acquire the skills he needs to move ahead in the field?

_____

_____

_____

_____

Author and speaker Chip Conley, author of *PEAK: How Great Companies Get Their Mojo from Maslow*, makes a distinction between people who have a job, and those who have a career: "Those with *jobs* tend to focus more on the financial rewards of working than on any pleasure or fulfillment," he writes. "Those with *careers* focus primarily on growing their talent and advancement."

When I think about that distinction as it might be applied to training, it occurs to me that there may be a difference between someone who does training for a living and a "training professional." A trainer who has achieved a certain level of skill and experience can do a perfectly competent job day after day, year after year. But for that person to see training as a career means becoming a training professional—someone who continues to learn, develop, and grow. To become, in the immortal words of the U.S. Army, the best that he or she can be.

In the first chapter of this book, you learned about the qualities and characteristics that successful trainers share. In this chapter you'll learn about:

- What distinguishes a training professional
- How to become a training professional
- Strategies for learning more about training and becoming a trainer
- How to create a professional development plan

If you like being a trainer, don't stop there. Be a master trainer. Be a respected, knowledgeable trainer. Be a successful trainer. Be a highly professional trainer. Be all the things that you are capable of being. Astound yourself!

Elaine Biech, "Lifelong Learning,"
in T. Garguilo (Ed.), *The Trainer's Portable Mentor*

1. What Distinguishes a Training Professional

THINK ABOUT IT

"Professional" is one of those words we often use without thinking much about what it means. Is it doing something for money instead of for fun? Going to work in a suit instead of in overalls? Having a degree or a title? How would you define the word "professional"?

_____

_____

Dictionary definitions of the word "professional" are somewhat broad. One definition is "participating for gain or livelihood in an activity or field of endeavor often engaged in by amateurs." But that definition would leave out a lot of people, such as winemakers, community volunteers, and artists who do what they do primarily because they love it, yet are consummate professionals in terms of their skill, knowledge, attention, and dedication. (Chip Conley would say that those people have a "calling" because "they consider the work itself fulfilling in its own right, without regard to money or advancement.")

Training Fundamentals: Pfeiffer Essential Guides to Training Basics.
Copyright © 2010 by John Wiley & Sons, Inc.
Reproduced by permission of Pfeiffer, an Imprint of Wiley. www.Pfeiffer.com

For a person to be considered a training professional, I would venture to say that he or she should have these characteristics:

- *A career focus.* We all need to bring in enough money so we can survive and prosper—pay for our housing, transportation, and clothing, buy groceries, educate our children, and take a vacation once in a while. But training professionals are people for whom training is more than a paycheck. They find satisfaction in being good at what they do, continually developing their skills and abilities, advancing in the field, and being part of the training community.

- *Knowledgeable.* Like other professionals, training professionals keep themselves informed about new developments and trends in the field. They are continually seeking out best practices and new methodologies—anything that might help them do a better job.

- *Passion for learning.* You already know that one key characteristic that trainers share is an enthusiasm for learning. It might be that training professionals are more than enthusiastic—they *love* to learn. When they've mastered something, they move on to something new. They see learning as a lifelong pursuit.

- *Purposeful.* Like other professionals, people who see training as their life's work are not satisfied with doing a competent job. They want to do the very best they can. They build on their successes and learn from their mistakes with the goal of designing and delivering the best training possible.

- *Innovative.* Training professionals welcome challenges, seeing them as opportunities to go beyond the traditional ways of thinking and the obvious constraints so they can come up with new and better approaches.

- *Reliable and trustworthy.* Training professionals earn the trust and respect of their colleagues, their managers and clients, and their learners because they can be counted on to do what they say they are going to do. They meet their commitments as completely and as well as possible. They keep confidential information to themselves and respect the work of others, giving credit where credit is due.

2. How to Become a Training Professional

Developing yourself as a training professional is not all that different from developing a training program: First, assess where you are now and determine where you are going. Examine the gaps to identify what you need to know and be able to do to achieve your objectives. Develop an action plan that includes areas on which to focus, action steps, a timetable, and a way to measure your progress. You began the process in Chapter 1, when you assessed your strengths and challenges.

Identifying What You Bring to the Field

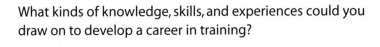

THINK ABOUT IT

What kinds of knowledge, skills, and experiences could you draw on to develop a career in training?

_____

_____

_____

_____

People do not come to the training field as blank slates. Just as learners build on their prior knowledge, skills, and experience during a training program, the experience, expertise, and education that you bring to the field forms the foundation for your training career.

Some of your most valuable experiences come from your years as a student, where you learned how to learn—and where you also learned how to write, plan, organize, and manage your time. The jobs you have held required that you learn a variety of skills that are essential for a trainer, including how to communicate clearly, solve problems, and work with other people. You might have had opportunities to teach others, perhaps as a coach or an informal on-the-job trainer. In fact, because training intersects with so many different subjects and requires so many different skills, you'll find that much of what you've done and learned over your lifetime will prove valuable as you develop yourself as a training professional.

Here are some questions that can help you identify specific experiences that you can draw on for your career in training:

- *Do you have teaching experience?* It's not surprising that many people come to training from a career in education. Although training and education differ in significant ways (as you learned in Chapter 1), both careers require many of the same characteristics and skills. If you've been a teacher, think about what you learned from your experience that you can use as a training professional.

- *Have you been a coach or taught outside of the field of education?* Many people who haven't worked as teachers have still had opportunities to teach. Perhaps you coached a soccer team or tutored people with reading problems at your local library. You might have helped a new employee learn a new job or taught a teenager how to grill hamburgers. All those experiences can help you as a trainer.

- *What courses have you taken in subjects that are related to training?* As a training professional, you'll draw on everything you've learned in college classes, workshops, and seminars about adult education, instructional design, presentation skills, project management, communication skills, marketing, strategic planning, problem solving, and a vast range of other topics. Think about what you've learned and how it will be useful to you as a trainer.

- *Do you have experience as a public speaker?* Trainers spend a lot of their time speaking to groups. Any experience you have had making presentations or speeches, whether related to work or in non-work situations, will be invaluable.

- *Do you have expertise in a specific subject area?* Perhaps you have had a previous career in health care, insurance, working with the disabled, accounting, environmental engineering, or another field. You can draw on that expertise to pursue training opportunities. For example, if you have worked as a nurse, an obvious opportunity would be training in the health care field. Think about areas in which you might like to specialize and ways in which you can use your expertise to further your training career.

- *What are you good at and what do you enjoy doing?* We're all so different. Some of us are good at analyzing and writing, some at art or music; some like to perform and some like to build things; some are excellent critics, some delight in solving problems. Each of us brings our own unique abilities to the training profession, and the profession offers lots of opportunities for us to draw on our talents and explore our interests. Think about the ways in which your talents and areas of interest can contribute to your development as a professional trainer.

● ●

THINK ABOUT IT

What experience, expertise, and education form the foundation for your training career?

❏   Teaching experience?

_____

_____

❏   Adult education, instructional design, or other courses related to training?

_____

_____

❏   Public speaking experience?

_____

_____

❏   Expertise in a specific subject area?

_____

_____

❏   Talents and areas of interest?

_____

_____

❏   Other?

_____

_____

● ●

3. Strategies for Learning More

Check What You Know

What are some ways in which you can learn more about the training field and continue your development? Where can you turn for information and resources? What steps can you take to develop your skills?

_____

_____

_____

_____

_____

_____

Once you have a good idea of where you are now, you can determine what gaps you need to close to get to where you want to be. Luckily, you're embarking on a journey that many people have taken—and not just any people, but people whose professional focus is helping others learn. There is a vast amount of information available in books and on the web. You can choose from many different university programs, seminars, workshops, and web-based learning programs on many different topics related to the field. Communities of training professionals are wonderful resources for ideas, information, and support.

Here are some specific steps you can take to learn more about the training field and develop your skills.

- *Seek opportunities to learn.* Build on the foundation that you bring to the field by taking courses that improve or expand your skills and knowledge. University extension programs and community colleges, professional associations, and private companies offer a wide range of courses on presentation skills, facilitation skills, training techniques, communication skills, instructional design, training-related technology, and other important topics. An increasing number of courses are offered online or in virtual classrooms.

- *Stay informed about current events, best practices, and trends in the field.* A great deal of training-related information is now available for download, and much of it is free. Subscribe to podcasts, webcasts, and newsletters that will keep you up-to-date with what's happening in the field and provide ideas that you can use in your work.

- *Get in the habit of reading.* Most training professionals hate moving their offices because they have so many books. There are hundreds of excellent books and articles available on training and related topics. You can use the suggested resources at the back of this book to started building a library of your own. Ask colleagues what books they've found useful. Search Amazon and other online bookstores for topics that interest you. Read a variety of perspectives on the various theories about the ways in which people learn and the different approaches to the instructional design process. Collect books with suggestions for activities so they'll be right at hand while you're designing, developing, or preparing for a training program. Keep your eye out for new publications that offer new information or insights.

- *Get a degree.* If you are serious about making training your career, you might want to go back to school. The coursework required for a degree in a field such as adult education, training and development, organization development, or instructional technology will expand your knowledge and skills, and a degree can make you more competitive. Many colleges and universities offer such programs in their extension divisions, and you might be able to attend classes at night, on weekends, or even online. Your company might have a program that pays all or part of the cost.

- *Become certified.* Being certified means that you have demonstrated the ability to meet certain criteria—that you are qualified to perform the required tasks and responsibilities required to perform a job or task. Certification helps you in two important ways: you acquire valuable knowledge and learn valuable skills, and you improve your ability to be taken seriously as a training professional. Completing a reputable certification program from a recognized organization such as ASTD or the Bob Pike Group can increase your confidence and credibility and make you more competitive in the job market.

- *Become active in the training community.* Other training professionals are your best resources for information, ideas, best practices, and support. Active memberships in professional organizations such as the American Society for Training and Development (ASTD) help you keep up with the newest developments in the field, find learning opportunities, and develop the relationships with other training professionals that will be important to your success. See the Resources section in the back of this book for a list of organizations.

- *Go to conferences.* The conferences held by professional organizations and industry-specific training groups are excellent sources of information about training trends and strategies. The social events offer opportunities to network with training professionals from all over the world; the panels and workshops offer many different learning opportunities. You can also share what you know, practice your craft, and become known in the field by volunteering to sit on panels and conduct workshops.

- *Find a mentor.* Many successful people attribute much of their success to the help and support of people who were sincerely interested in helping them develop their careers. Establish a relationship with an experienced training professional you respect who is willing to give you help and support as you develop your career.

- *Observe other trainers in action.* Many training professionals have learned what they know by watching other trainers at work. Look for opportunities to participate in or observe workshops delivered by trainers who've been in the field for a while. Notice what they do to get started, engage participants, manage the group, and use activities. Ask questions about what you see and about the strategies they find useful to keep workshops on track and help people learn.

- *Create opportunities to apply your skills.* Just as participants in a training program need practice so they can apply what they learn, you need practice that helps you apply what you learn about training. Volunteer to work on training projects, especially those that give you a chance to work alongside more experienced training professionals as they design and deliver training. Ask other trainers whether you can assist in their workshops; offer to be part of an instructional design team. Volunteer to help a nonprofit group develop a training program for its staff. Conduct workshops for a community group or the local chapter of a professional organization.

To Learn More and Develop Your Skills

- Take courses on topics related to the training field that help you improve your skills and expand your knowledge.
- Stay informed about best practices and new developments in the field by subscribing to podcasts, webcasts, and newsletters.
- Build a library of books and articles on training-related topics and get in the habit of reading.
- Get a degree in a field that's related to training.
- Become certified.
- Become active in the training community.
- Attend conferences.
- Find a mentor.
- Observe other trainers in action.
- Volunteer to apply your skills as a trainer.

4. Making a Professional Development Plan

THINK ABOUT IT

Have you ever developed an action plan to help you carry out a project or achieve a specific goal? What components did the plan have? How did you use it? What purpose did it serve?

_____

_____

_____

_____

_____

_____

Planning is a process for getting us from where we are to where we want to be. Deciding that you would like to take a trip to a foreign city is only the first step—there are a lot of tasks to accomplish before you can arrive at that destination. As you've learned in this book, the idea that training is needed is only the first step in developing a training program—there are many tasks to accomplish and many decisions to make along the way. Similarly, deciding that you want to build a career as a professional trainer is only the first step. Reaching that goal requires thinking carefully about what your destination really is and what you need to do to get there. It requires making a professional development plan.

Personal development planning is a type of action planning. Organizations use action plans—strategic planning—to help them identify and achieve their strategic goals. Teams use action plans—project planning—to identify, schedule, and manage all the tasks needed to carry out a project. Learners use action plans to transfer what they have learned to the workplace. In the same way, training professionals use action plans to help them achieve their career goals.

In its simplest form, an action plan is a list of what you need to do to achieve a specific goal, the resources you will need, and deadlines for taking or completing actions. The process of developing an action plan forces you to think through what you will do and how you are going to do it. A good action plan helps you stay on track, spot problems early, and respond to changing needs and situations; it also serves as a checklist for monitoring your progress.

To Make the Best Use of Action Plans

- Limit the number and complexity of objectives you try to achieve at one time.
- Be realistic and flexible.
- Tell someone about your plan.
- Focus on action steps and set deadlines.
- When you achieve a goal, make a new plan and start again.

For any action plan to achieve its purpose, which is to help you accomplish specific goals, it needs to be realistic. An action plan that includes too many tasks and too many objectives is likely to promote procrastination instead of action because it is too overwhelming. If the timetable is unrealistic or essential resources are unavailable, the action plan is more likely to lead to frustration than to success.

The best action plans are focused and realistic, limited to only a few achievable objectives at a time. Action plans are also more useful when they are shared with other people.

Here are some suggestions for making the best use of action plans:

- *Limit the number and complexity of objectives you try to achieve at one time.* If you try to do too much, chances are you won't do much of anything. If a goal is to improve your presentation skills, focus on that for a while instead of trying to learn how to develop e-learning programs at the same time. Take one small step at a time and let small successes propel you forward.

- *Be realistic and flexible.* Consider the amount of time you can devote to working toward a goal, and how much you can realistically accomplish within a given amount of time. Revise your action plan if things change. No matter what your intentions, you can't control everything. If you need to change a deadline, change it. If you need to add a step, add it. If resources you need are not available, come up with some options. If the goal changes, do a new action plan.

- *Tell someone about your plan.* Sharing, or "publishing," your action plan helps to reinforce your commitment. You can review your plan and discuss your goals with a friend, a colleague, your manager, or anyone else with whom you feel comfortable.

- *Focus on action steps and set deadlines.* Once you identify a goal, determine what actions you can take to achieve it. Set a deadline for each action. Consider the actions for achieving a goal among your top priorities.

- *When you achieve your goals, set new ones.* First, reward yourself for your hard work and accomplishments. Then choose new goals and make a new action plan. Do it again, and again. One of the things that makes training such an exciting field is that there is always more to discover, more to learn. As Elaine Biech said in the quote earlier in this chapter: *"Astound yourself!"*

Your Professional Development Plan

To know that you have reached a destination, you first need to know what that destination looks like: "There's the Eiffel Tower—this must be Paris!" Making a professional development plan starts with describing your destination—the situation that will exist when you have achieved your goals. Once you have a clear picture of the destination, then you can figure out the best way to get there.

Think about your long-term career goal: Is there a subject area in which you would like to specialize? An area of training in which you would like to become an expert? Are you interested more in designing and developing programs than in delivering them, or the other way around? Would you like to focus on technology-based training?

Your long-term career goals are likely to change over time, as you gain more experience and knowledge about the training world, as new opportunities present themselves, and the training world itself changes. It's important to reassess your goals from time to time so that you can make whatever adjustments might be needed in your action planning process.

THINK ABOUT IT

How do you see your role in the training world five years from now? Imagine that you are about to give a presentation for a group of university students who are considering training as a career. Write three sentences that the professor would say to introduce you.

_____

_____

_____

_____

_____

_____

To develop an action plan for reaching your ultimate destination, you need to think about what you already know and are able to do. This analysis process is similar to the first stage of ADDIE—the purpose is to identify the gap between the current situation and the desired outcome.

THINK ABOUT IT

Look back at the assessment you completed in Chapter 1 and your answers to the questions in this chapter.

1. What strengths do you bring to the field of training that will help you achieve your professional goals?

_____

_____

_____

_____

2. What are your challenges?

_____

_____

_____

_____

3. What experience, education, and expertise do you have that can contribute to your career?

_____

_____

_____

_____

Apply What You Learn

Use the worksheet on the next page to make an action plan for yourself. When you have finished your action plan, share it with someone else—a colleague, a mentor, a manager, or a friend. When you have achieved your objective, reward yourself—and then make a new plan.

Action Planning Worksheet

Today's date: _____

What is your long-term goal? (Field in which you would like to specialize? Area of training in which you would like to become an expert?) In three sentences, describe what you will be doing five years from now.

_____

_____

_____

_____

_____

_____

Choose one to three objectives on which to focus during the next three to six months:

Objective 1:

_____

_____

_____

_____

Objective 2:

_____

_____

_____

_____

(Continued)

Objective 3:

_____

_____

_____

_____

What actions will you take to achieve your objective? When will you take each action?

Actions	Dates
Objective 1	
Objective 2	
Objective 3	

Where can you find resources, help, and support for achieving your objectives?

Resources for Objective 1:

_____

_____

Resources for Objective 2:

_____

_____

Resources for Objective 3:

_____

_____

What rewards will you give yourself when you accomplish your objectives?

_____

_____

When you have accomplished your objectives, choose new ones and make a new action plan.

Resources

The publications, websites, and associations on this list are only a few of the excellent resources available for learning more about training. You can find books that are out of print at Amazon.com and other online booksellers. Also check out www.HRDPress.com, www.AMACOM.com, and www.Pfeiffer.com for other great training resources.

Publications

Allen, Michael. *Michael Allen's 2009 e-Learning Annual*. San Francisco: Pfeiffer, 2009.

ASTD. *2007 State of the Industry Report*. Alexandria, VA: Author. (www.astd.org)

ASTD. *2004 Competency Model*. Alexandria, VA: Author. (www.astd.org)

Barbazette, Jean. *The Art of Great Training Delivery: Strategies, Tools, and Tactics*. San Francisco: Pfeiffer, 2006.

Biech, Elaine (Ed.). *90 World-Class Activities by 90 World-Class Trainers*. San Francisco: Pfeiffer, 2007.

Biech, Elaine. *Training for Dummies*. Hoboken, NJ: John Wiley & Sons, 2005.

Bloom, Benjamin S. *Taxonomy of Educational Objectives*. Boston: Allyn and Bacon, 1984.

Bowman, Sharon L. *Training from the Back of the Room!: 65 Ways to Step Aside and Let Them Learn*. San Francisco: Pfeiffer, 2008.

Caffarella, Rosemary S. *Planning Programs for Adult Learners* (2nd ed.). San Francisco: Jossey-Bass, 2002.

Clark, Ruth Colvin, and Kwinn, Ann. *The New Virtual Classroom: Evidence-Based Guidelines for Synchronous e-Learning*. San Francisco: Pfeiffer, 2007.

Clark, Ruth Colvin, and Mayer, Richard E. *e-Learning and the Science of Instruction* (2nd ed.). San Francisco: Pfeiffer, 2008.

Conley, Chip. *PEAK: How Great Companies Get Their Mojo from Maslow*. San Francisco: Jossey-Bass, 2007.

Covey, Stephen R. *7 Habits of Highly Effective People*. New York: Simon and Schuster, 2004.

Diamond, Robert M. *Designing and Assessing Courses and Curricula*. San Francisco: Jossey-Bass, 1998.

Fee, Kenneth. *Delivering e-Learning: A Complete Strategy for Design, Application, and Assessment*. London: Kogan-Page, 2009.

Foshay, Wellesley; Silver, Kenneth; and Stelnicki, Michael. *Writing Training Materials That Work: How to Train Anyone to Do Anything*. San Francisco: Pfeiffer, 2003.

Gardner, Howard. *Multiple Intelligences: New Horizons in Theory and Practice*. New York: Basic Books, 2006.

Gargiulo, Terrence L. *Once Upon a Time: Using Story-Based Activities to Develop Breakthrough Communication Skills*. San Francisco, Pfeiffer, 2007.

Gargiulo, Terrence L., Pangarkar, Ajay M., and Teresa Kirkwood. *The Trainer's Portable Mentor*. San Francisco: Pfeiffer, 2008.

Goad, Tom W. *The First-Time Trainer*. New York: AMACOM, 1997.

Goman, Carol Kinsey. *The Nonverbal Advantage: Secrets and Science of Body Language at Work*. San Francisco: Berrett-Koehler, 2008.

Gronstedt, Anders. Training in Virtual Worlds: Training Technology and e-Learning. *Infoline, 25*. Alexandria, VA: ASTD, 2008.

Gupta, Kavita. *A Practical Guide to Needs Assessment* (2nd ed.). San Francisco: Pfeiffer, 2007.

Hodell, Chuck. *ISD from the Ground Up: A No-Nonsense Approach to Instructional Design* (2nd ed.). Alexandria, VA: ASTD, 2006.

Kirkpatrick, Donald L., and Kirkpatrick, James D. *Evaluating Training Programs: The Four Levels* (3rd ed.). San Francisco: Berrett-Koehler, 2006.

Knowles, Malcolm S., Holton III, Elwood F., and Swanson, Richard A. *The Adult Learner: The Definitive Classic in Adult Education and Human Resource Development* (6th ed.). Amsterdam: Elsevier, 2005.

Kolb, David A. *Experiential Learning: Experience as the Source of Learning and Development*. Upper Saddle River, NJ: Prentice-Hall, 1984.

Lawson, Karen. *The Trainer's Handbook* (2nd ed.). San Francisco: Pfeiffer, 2006 (updated edition, 2008).

Leatherman, Dick. *Training Trilogy: Conducting Needs Assessment, Designing Programs, Training Skills* (3rd ed.). Amherst, MA: HRD Press, 2007.

Leigh, David. *The Group Trainer's Handbook: Designing and Delivering Training for Groups* (3rd ed.). London: Kogan-Page, 2006.

Mager, Robert F. *Preparing Instructional Objectives* (2nd ed.). Belmont, CA: David Lake Publishers, 1984.

Nadler, Leonard. *The Handbook of Human Resource Development*. Hoboken, NJ: John Wiley & Sons, 1984.

Pike, Robert W. *Creative Training Techniques Handbook: Tips, Tactics, and How-To's for Delivering Effective Training* (3rd ed.). Amherst, MA: HRD Press, 2003.

Silberman, Mel. *Training the Active Way*. San Francisco: Pfeiffer, 2006.

Society for Human Resource Management (SHRM). *2006 Workplace Forecast*. Alexandria, VA: Author. (www.shrm.org)

Stolovitch, Harold D., and Keeps, Erica J. *Telling Ain't Training*. Alexandria, VA: ASTD, 2002.

Thiagarajan, Sivasailam. *Thiagi's Interactive Lectures*. Alexandria, VA: ASTD, 2005.

Thorne, Kaye, and Mackey, David. *Everything You Ever Needed to Know About Training* (4th ed.). London: Kogan Page, 2007.

Weimer, Maryellen. *Learner-Centered Teaching*. San Francisco: Jossey-Bass, 2002.

Wilder, Claudyne. *Point, Click & Wow!: The Techniques and Habits of Successful Presenters* (3rd ed.). San Francisco: Pfeiffer, 2008.

Magazines, Websites, and Newsletters

Websites and the addresses of web publications change frequently. If you are unable to find a magazine, website, or newsletter using the web address on this list, try a web search for an updated address.

Accelerated Learning Network Newsletter: www.accelerated-learning.net

ASTD Learning Circuits articles: www.astd.org/lc

Creative Training Techniques Newsletter: www.creativetrainingtech.com

Don Clark/Big Dog, Little Dog: nwlink.com/~donclark, bdld.blogspot.com/

eLearn Magazine: www.elearnmag.org

Ignite Newsletter: www.kenblanchard.com/Business_Leadership/Management_Leadership_Newsletter/

www.intulogy.com/library

Learning at Light Speed weblog: www.learningatlightspeed.com

Performance Improvement Journal (PIJ): www.ispi.org (resource center)

Peter Honey and Alan Mumford's Learning Styles Questionnaire, www.peterhoney.com

www.roiinstitute.net

Training and Development: www.astd.org/TD/

Training magazine, Lakewood Publishers: www.trainingmag.com

Associations and Organizations

These associations and organizations are excellent resources for people in the training field, offering information, learning opportunities, publications, blogs, conferences, networking, and more.

American Society for Training and Development (ASTD), www.astd.org/

American Management Association (AMA), www.amanet.org

The e-Learning Guild, www.elearningguild.com

International Association of Facilitators (IAF), www.iaf-world.org

International Society for Performance Improvement (ISPI), www.ispi.org

Society for Human Resource Management (SHRM), www.shrm.org

About the Author

Janis Fisher Chan, a writer, editor, instructional designer, and trainer, has been in the training field for more than twenty-five years. As a co-founder of Write It Well (formerly Advanced Communication Designs), a training company that specializes in helping people communicate clearly and work together productively, she designed and conducted a wide range of training programs on topics that ranged from business writing to negotiating and consulted with clients on training-related issues. She is the author of *E-Mail: A Write It Well Guide—How to Write and Manage E-Mail in the Workplace* and other books in the Write It Well series; Pfeiffer's *An Academic Manager's Guide to Meetings*; and the American Management Association's self-study courses *How to Manage Your Priorities* (2nd ed.); *Delegating for Business Success; Presentation Success*; and *Communication Skills for Managers* (5th ed.). She also served as an instructional writer and developmental editor for the highly acclaimed *Leadership Challenge Workshop, The Five Dysfunctions of a Team* Workshop Kit, and other books and training packages for Pfeiffer and other publishers. After receiving her master's degree in theater from San Francisco State University, she returned to the university to complete a post-graduate program in organization development. She lives in Marin County, California.

Index

Auditory learners, 39, 206
Authoring tool, 206
Avatar, 206

B

Barbazette, J., 124
Baseline, 206
Behavioral objectives, 206
Beta testing, 140–141, 151
Biech, E., 14, 180, 217
Blended learning, 98, 206
Bloom, B., 43
Bloom's Taxonomy, 43, 207
Bodily-kinesthetic intelligence, 40
Bowman, S., 31, 117
Breakout room, 207

C

Caffarella, R., 48
Case study, 207
Change: needs assessment to identify need and outcome, 58; recognizing training role in, 59–60; root cause-current situation gap and, 58–59; training to manage, 8
Check What You Know icon: about training, 1–2; analysis process, 56, 65–66, 75; becoming a training professional, 215–216, 222; concerns about implementing program, 159; delivery options, 83, 89, 99, 105, 106–108; designing training programs, 47; developing vs. purchasing program, 115, 148; development tasks, 113, 148; experiential learning, 129, 150; giving workshops, 198–199; instructional design process, 49; learning activities, 125; learning objectives, 68, 77; learning styles and training, 41; matching learning activity to program type, 149; preparing participants for training, 166; program evaluation, 142; room setups, 172, 199; running the workshop, 192; structuring training programs, 131, 150; teaching adults, 23–24; testing the program, 140; training requests and urgency, 74; training

terminology, 203–204; what content to include, 118; what makes a "good" trainer, 11–12; what the development tasks are, 111; what trainers do, 9; why organizations need training, 6; workshop opening, 133, 151; workshop preparation, 162, 182
Child learners, 29t
Chunking, 207
Classroom style setup, 175
Cognitive (knowledge) domain, 43
Cognitive skills, 207
Collaborative learning, 207
Collaborative skills, 15, 16
Comfort factor, 178
Communication skills, 13
Competency, 207
Competency model, 207
Computer-based training (CBT), 207
Conceptualizing (or processing), 130
Confirmation of reservations, 180–182
Connecting (or generalizing), 131
Content: creating sequence of, 132; definition of, 207; identifying and organizing the, 117–119; using learning objectives to select, 118–124, 149. *See also* Learning activities
Contingency plans, 180–182
Courseware, 207
Covey, S., 58
Creative Training Techniques (Pike), 4, 130, 167, 184
Creativity, 14
"Creativity, Emergence, and the Design of Learning Experiences" (Honebein), 113
Criterion-referenced instruction, 208
Cross-training, 208
Cultural differences, 7
Current situation-root cause gap, 58–59
Customer service training, 8

D

Declarative knowledge, 43
Deductive learning, 208
Delivery. *See* Training delivery
Demographics, 208

Knowledge: declarative vs. procedural, 43; domain of cognitive, 43
Knowles, M., 31
Kolb, D., 37
KSAs (Knowledge, Skills, and Attitude), 43, 207

L

Language of training: acronyms, 212; glossary of, 205–213; importance of learning the, 205; importance of understanding, 203–205
Learner-Centered Teaching (Weimer), 25, 30
Learner-centered training: comparing trainer-centered and, 25–28, 33–34; description of, 29–30; how trainers use, 31–32, 35; room setups conveying, 199
Learning: accelerated, 205–206; action, 206; andragogy approach to, 31, 206; blended, 98, 206; deductive, 208; discovery, 208; distance, 208; experiential, 129–131, 150, 208; inductive, 209; real-world situation applications of, 34; self-directed, 211; successful trainer's enthusiasm for, 13–14; traditional pedagogical model of, 31. *See also* Adult learning
Learning activities: ADA Approach (learners do an activity) to, 130; developing, 124, 129; experiential learning through, 129–131, 150, 208; guidelines for selecting, 128; matching training program type to, 149; role play, 210; structuring the program, 131–133; types of, 126–127. *See also* Content
Learning collaborative, 207
Learning domains, 43
Learning management system (LMS), 210
Learning objectives: check what you know about, 68, 77; content development guided by, 118–124, 149; definition of, 210; enabling objective and, 208; identifying descriptive words for, 70–71; importance of writing, 67; practice for rewriting, 72; thinking about what makes good, 69, 70–72, 77–78; as training delivery consideration, 100; training design enabling, 73; Training Program Design Planning Worksheet on, 79–82

Learning programs: asynchronous, 86, 87–88t, 206; blended learning, 98, 206; decision to develop, adapt, or purchase, 115–117; off-the-shelf, 115–117, 148, 210; on-the-job training, 95–96; podcasts, 96, 97, 137, 210; self-directed e-Learning, 94, 137; self-paced print, 93, 137, 211; study groups, 95; synchronous, 86, 87, 88t, 211; videos, 97, 137. *See also* Training programs
Learning styles: differences in, 36–37; four primary, 37–38; how they impact training, 41–42; learner-centered training approach to, 32; multiple intelligences and, 39–40; three primary sensory receivers and, 38–39. *See also* Adult learning; Participants
Learning Styles Questionnaire, 37
Learning types: differences in, 42; three learning domains and, 43
"Lifelong Learning" (Biech), 217
Live in-person workshops: matching topics to, 108; materials for, 137; overview of, 90–91; virtual vs., 92, 109
Logical-mathematical intelligence, 39

M

Mager, R. F., 60, 69, 71
Managers training preferences, 102
Mandated training issues, 64
Materials. *See* Training materials
Mentors, 224
Motivation, 28
Multiple intelligences, 39–40, 210
Mumford, A., 37
Murray, R., 161
Musical intelligence, 40

N

Nadler, L., 3
Naturalist intelligence, 40
Needs assessments: during analysis stage of ADDIE model, 55; definition of, 210; to identify training need and outcome, 58; of learners' needs and characteristics, 63–64; on root cause-current situation gap, 58–59; trainer role in, 10. *See also* Training needs

Nervousness, 190

Training programs: analysis and planning for, 52–66, 75; asynchronous, 86, 87–88*t*, 206; characteristics of successful, 5; deciding length of, 119; designing, 47–82; needs filled by, 10; purchasing vs. developing, 115–117, 148; selecting delivery methods for, 73, 74, 83–109; synchronous, 86, 87, 88*t*, 211; trainer's role in developing, 9–10; writing learning objectives for, 67–74. *See also* Learning programs; Training

Training skills: communication, 13; creating opportunities to apply, 224; development of your, 225; professional development plan to increase, 225–229

U

U-shaped conference table, 177
University of Chicago, 43
U.S. Department of Defense, 51

V

Validation, 212
Verbal-linguistic intelligence, 39
Videos, 97, 137
Virtual workshops: description of, 91–92; live in-person vs., 92, 109; materials for, 137
Visual, Auditory, and Kinesthetic (VAK) model, 38–39
Visual learners, 38–39, 212–213
Vodcast, 213
Voiceover internet protocol (VoIP), 213

W

Web-based training (WBT), 213
Webinar, 213
Websites: ASTD, 15; Steven Covey, 58
Weimer, M., 25, 30
"Welcome" e-mail, 168
WIIFM (What's in it for me?), 28

Wiki, 213
Workforce learning professional, 213
Worksheets: Action Planning, 231–232; Adapt, Purchase, or Develop?, 152–155; Planning and Preparing for a Workshop, 200–201; Training Program Design Planning, 79–82
Workshop Material Checklist, 179
Workshop opening: comparing good and poor, 185; considering effective approaches to, 151; functions served by, 133–134; guidelines for, 186–192; icebreakers during, 189, 209
Workshop preparation: confirming arrangement/making contingency plans, 180–182; equipment related, 165, 178, 182; facility related, 164–165, 180–181; getting ready to conduct training, 183–184; overview of tasks for, 163; Planning and Preparing for a Workshop Worksheet, 200–201; pre-work assignments to participants, 170–171; pre-workshop questionnaire, 169; room setups, 172, 173–180, 199; sample "Welcome" e-mail, 168; scheduling the training, 163–165; ways to prepare participants, 166–167
Workshops: comparing traditional and virtual, 92, 109; comparing well prepared/poorly prepared, 185; concerns related to giving the, 159–161; getting started, 184–192; opening and closing, 133–134, 151; preparation before the, 162–184; Quick Quiz on, 197; running the, 192–197; traditional live in-person, 90–91, 92, 108, 109, 137; virtual, 91–92, 109, 137
Writing Training Materials That Work (Foshay, Silber, and Stelnicki), 28

Y

YCDI (You can do it), 28